(continued)

Young Investigators

THE PROJECT APPROACH IN THE EARLY YEARS

JUDY HARRIS HELM
LILIAN G. KATZ

TEACHERS COLLEGE PRESS

Teachers College, Columbia University
New York and London

Author's Note: Thanks to Rebecca Cowser for the photo on our cover. The two children are from her kindergarten class at Little Friends Learning Center. They are sketching while on a field site visit during the Farm Project.

Published by Teachers College Press, 1234 Amsterdam Avenue, New York, NY 10027

Library of Congress Cataloging-in-Publication Data

Helm, Judy Harris.
    Young investigators : the project approach in the early years / Judy Harris Helm, Lilian G. Katz.
        p. cm. — (Early childhood education series)
    Includes bibliographical references and index.
    ISBN 0-8077-4016-0 (pbk. : alk. paper)
    1. Project method in teaching.   2. Early childhood education—Curricula.
I. Katz, Lilian.   II. Title.   III. Early childhood education series (Teachers College Press)
LB1139.35.P8 H46 2000
372.13'6—dc21   00-057741

ISBN 0-8077-4016-0 (paper)

Printed on acid-free paper
Manufactured in the United States of America

07   8   7   6   5

To our husbands, Richard Helm and Boris Katz, who have supported and encouraged us to take our own journeys and do our own project work; and to the teachers and children who have opened their classrooms and minds and by whom we have been instructed, inspired, and enriched.

Contents

Preface

This book was written in response to questions raised and issues presented as we have worked with many teachers over years to help them implement the project approach.

In the course of this work many questions were asked about how best to involve in project work young children who had not yet achieved mastery of basic literacy skills. Many resources for teachers that are currently available on the project approach are most useful for older children who have verbal fluency. These children, who often have a large vocabulary, can easily talk about their previous experiences with a topic and formulate questions for investigation. In addition, mastery of literacy skills (reading and writing) provides older children with ways of researching the topic, recording their thoughts, and representing their growing understanding of the topic, all of which are not usually part of the young child's repertoire. Children who are 3 and 4 years old are still developing verbal fluency and the ability to organize their thoughts for communication. Formulating questions for investigation is often a challenge for young children. Five- and 6-year-olds are in the process of learning what the reading and writing process is all about. Research and representation take a different direction with these young learners. In addition, children with special needs in classrooms often present communication and representation challenges for project work. This book provides another resource that specifically addresses some of these issues.

In our work with teachers we have also encountered doubts about whether children whose early experiences seemed to put them at risk for difficulties in school might respond to the exploratory and child-initiated nature of project work. In such cases also, many school officials and teachers expressed the conviction that children coming to school with less than optimal school readiness and from low-income homes were most in need of formal academic exercises, and that experiences like project work were most appropriate for wealthy and gifted children. As if these kinds of concerns were not sufficient to inhibit teachers' temptations to try project work in their curriculum, recent developments have placed them under increasing pressure to meet state and local performance and content standards. Many educators believe that such standards cannot be addressed in any way other than formal instruction. These concerns are addressed throughout this book.

Interest in the project approach has been growing fairly consistently in the last decade as more and more teachers have reported their experiences in journals, at conferences, and on the Project Approach Listserv offered by the ERIC Clearinghouse on Elementary and Early Childhood Education <PROJECTS-L@POSTOFFICE. CSO.UIUC.EDU>. Another major influence on educators of the under 7-year-olds has been exposure to a great deal of information about the cutting-edge developments in early childhood education in the small northern Italian City of Reggio Emilia, including the extended projects done by the young children. The approach to project work taken in Reggio Emilia is more informal and flexible than the strategies we recommend and describe (see Hendricks, 1997). Nevertheless, all of us in the field have been inspired and motivated by examining their work, especially in the use of "graphic languages" and the power of careful documentation to enrich the work of young children and their teachers.

Finally, this book is dedicated to the proposition that all children are natural-born investigators. Our experience confirms the related proposition that the preschool years are an ideal time to support and strengthen the inborn dispositions of all children to observe and to investigate their experience and environments by incorporating the project approach in the early childhood curriculum. As readers will realize throughout the following chapters, our confidence in this proposition is supported by a wide range of experiences with teachers and children by whom we have also been instructed, inspired, and enriched.

Acknowledgments

We are deeply indebted to our good colleagues, past co-authors, and personal friends, Sylvia Chard and Sallee Beneke, with whom we have each shared research and dialogue about projects. This book would not be possible without the extensive conversations and consultation with them that preceded the writing of this book. We are also grateful to the early childhood centers and schools where project work flourishes and inspires us, and whose work is included in this book. These include: Bing Nursery School, Don C. Parker Early Education Center, Holy Trinity Lutheran Church Preschool, Illinois State University Child Care Center, Little Friends Learning Center, St. Ambrose University Children's Campus, University Primary School at the University of Illinois, Valeska-Hinton Early Childhood Education Center, and Woodford County Special Education Association.

We are grateful to the staff at STARnet of Western Illinois University, especially Char Ward and Sharon Doubet, who have been tireless in their commitment to capturing and sharing the story of the Fire Truck Project in the accompanying video and in their *Apples Magazine* television program. STARnet has also provided support for training and dissemination. Jan Deissler and Brenda Smith of Child Care Connection at Illinois Central College have enabled many of the teachers in this book to learn about the project approach and documentation through their support of training and dissemination. We also want to thank the staff of the ERIC Clearinghouse on Elementary and Early Childhood Education for sharing reflections about projects and consistently encouraging our work.

In addition to the staff of the schools and centers listed above we want to acknowledge individually the competent, caring, and inspirational teachers who shared their experiences guiding projects and their children's work through personal interviews and documentation. These include Jolyn Blank, Scott Brouette, Judy Cagle, Mary Jane Elliott, Natalya Fehr, Barbara Gallick, Johnna Gerlach, Mary Ann Gottlieb, Ruth Harkema, Jean Lang, Lisa Lee, Linda Lundberg, Brenda Wiles, and Rebecca Wilson. They were all extremely generous in sharing their thoughts, their documentation, and their time. Cathy Wiggers shared her experiences as an administrator supporting projects. It is their work which will enable readers to see how projects can occur in real classrooms and can help teachers build the bridge between theory and implementation.

Special thanks go to Pam Scranton, the teacher who guided the Fire Truck Project. She videotaped the events in her classroom, preserved her thoughts in a written journal, and sat for hours of interviews. Chapter 7 is the story of the Fire Truck Project in Pam's own words assembled from these sources of documentation. We are grateful for her keen observations and her thoughtful reflection on the process. We learned much from Pam and are continually inspired by her commitment to learning and growing as a teacher.

Last but not least, we want to thank Susan Liddicoat and Karl Nyberg, our editors at Teachers College Press. Susan worked wonders with our words and nurtured us at the same time. Karl brought it all together. Their patience and encouragement enabled us to finish the task.

CHAPTER 1

Projects and Young Children

I just love to do projects with children because I think it is exciting watching them construct their own knowledge base . . . watching them decide what interests them the most, investigating it, asking questions about it. I like seeing children excited about what they're doing, excited about their learning. I like watching them almost on fire because they can't get the questions out fast enough and they can't get the materials in their hands fast enough to represent what they're learning as they investigate a topic. I think it is just the best way for children to grow and for their brains to develop.

—Pam Scranton, pre-kindergarten teacher

The project approach has captured the interest of early childhood teachers like Pam Scranton. Many teachers of young children have been challenged by the work of Lilian Katz and Sylvia Chard (2000; Chard, 1994) on the project approach to introduce opportunities for children to engage in investigation as part of the work undertaken in their classrooms. The early years are important years for all aspects of development. Children's natural dispositions to be intellectually curious and to investigate their environments emerge (Katz, 1995). They learn about tools such as reading and writing and become motivated to develop and use a wide variety of related skills. It is important that they have an opportunity to experience active, engaged learning.

However, research and investigations are easier to include in a curriculum for older students who have mastered reading and writing than in early childhood programs. This book presents the teaching strategies and project stories of Pam Scranton and other teachers who are successfully using the approach with 3-, 4-, and 5-year-olds and first graders who are beginning to read and write. We summarize the knowledge gained as projects were undertaken in schools, childcare centers, and early intervention programs in rural and urban areas, and in small towns. These projects are described with step-by-step explanations of how young children's projects are guided by teachers and caregivers.

THE PROJECT APPROACH

The project approach is not a new way to teach children (DuCharme, 1993). It was a central part of the Progressive Education movement and was used extensively in the British Infant Schools in the 1960s and 1970s (Smith, 1997). Interest in the potential value of project work was renewed with the publication in 1989 of the first edition of *Engaging Children's Minds: The Project Approach* (Katz & Chard). Even greater interest in it has been stimulated by the impressive reports and displays of group projects conducted by children in the pre-primary schools of Reggio Emilia (Edwards, Gandini, & Forman, 1993, 1998; Gandini, 1993; New, 1990, 1991; Rankin, 1992). According to Gandini (1997),

> Projects provide the backbone of the children's and teachers' learning experiences. They are based on the strong conviction that learning by doing is of great importance and that to discuss in group and to revisit ideas and experiences is the premier way of gaining better understanding and learning. (p. 7)

Although the word *project* has many meanings, when used in the "project approach," it has a specific meaning:

> A project is an in-depth investigation of a topic worth learning more about. The investigation is usually undertaken by a small group of children within a class, sometimes by a whole class, and occasionally by an individual child. The key feature of a project is that it is a research effort deliberately focused on finding answers to questions about a topic posed either by the children, the teacher, or the teacher working with the children. (Katz, 1994, p. 1)

Projects, Units, Themes, and Learning Centers

Many preschool and kindergarten teachers use units or themes for organizing the activities they provide. A theme is a broad concept or topic like "seasons" or "animals." When using a theme, teachers assemble books, photographs, and other materials related to the theme. Experiences in most content areas or domains of development (such as language, math, or science) relate or connect to the theme.

Units usually consist of preplanned lessons and activities on a specific topic that the teacher considers important for the children to know, such as "magnets" (Harlan, 1984). When providing information in units, the teacher typically has a clear plan about what concepts and knowledge he wants the children to learn.

Many preschool and kindergarten teachers also use learning centers as a way to organize their teaching. Areas of the room are designated for the investigation or development of certain knowledge and skills, such as "block area" or "music and movement area" (Dodge & Colker, 1992). Materials and equipment for each area are selected to teach concepts and provide practice in skills that the teacher wishes the children to develop.

In all these methods, however, the focus is not to help children pose questions to be answered or take the initiative for investigation. Many of these methods have an important place in the early childhood curriculum. However, there are additional opportunities for the growth of knowledge, skills, and dispositions when children ask their own questions, conduct their own investigations, and make decisions about their activities. Projects provide contexts in which children's curiosity can be expressed purposefully, and that enable them to experience the joy of self-motivated learning. Teachers don't always know what direction a project will take or what aspects of a topic will interest a particular group. Well-developed projects engage children's minds and emotions and become adventures that teachers and children embark on together.

The continuum in Figure 1.1 represents the degree of child initiation and decision making in the learning process in different approaches to teaching. Projects are on the far right of the continuum because a child or children in a classroom often initiate project topics. Projects also involve the child in making decisions about topic selection, investigation, and how to culminate the project. There are many valuable learning experiences that can and do occur at all points along the continuum. Teachers who use the project approach often also teach single concepts and utilize units, themes, and directed inquiry. Some topics, by their nature, do not make good project topics and are best taught as single concepts, units, or themes.

We believe, however, that projects provide experiences that involve students intellectually to a greater degree than the experiences that come from teacher-prepared units or themes. It is the children's initiative, involvement, and relative control over their own activities and participation in what is accomplished that distinguish projects from units or themes. Additional differences between projects and units or thematic teaching include the length of time devoted to the topic, the teacher's role, the timing of field trips, and the use of a variety of resources. These are summarized in Figure 1.2

Academic Tasks and Intellectual Goals

In understanding the role that projects play in an early childhood curriculum, it may be helpful to look at the difference between academic tasks and intellectual goals. Academic tasks are typically carefully structured, sequenced, and decontextualized small bits of information and discrete skills that often require some small-group or individual instruction by a knowledge-

Figure 1.1 Degree of child initiation and decision making in different approaches to teaching.

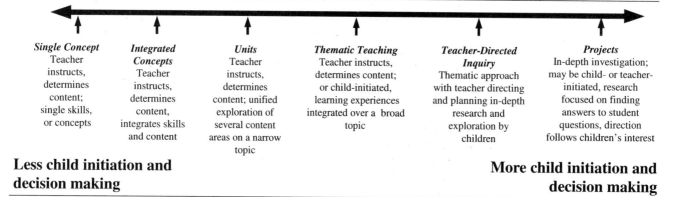

Single Concept	*Integrated Concepts*	*Units*	*Thematic Teaching*	*Teacher-Directed Inquiry*	*Projects*
Teacher instructs, determines content; single skills, or concepts	Teacher instructs, determines content, integrates skills and content	Teacher instructs, determines content; unified exploration of several content areas on a narrow topic	Teacher instructs, determines content; or child-initiated, learning experiences integrated over a broad topic	Thematic approach with teacher directing and planning in-depth research and exploration by children	In-depth investigation; may be child- or teacher-initiated, research focused on finding answers to student questions, direction follows children's interest

Less child initiation and decision making   **More child initiation and decision making**

Figure 1.2 Differences between teacher-planned experiences and the project approach.

In teacher-planned experiences like units you are more likely to see	In projects you are more likely to see
Length of learning experience predetermined, shorter time periods such as 1 or 2 weeks.	Length of learning experience determined by project progression, usually several weeks, sometimes months.
Topics determined by curriculum and teacher, may or may not be of interest to student.	Topics negotiated between students and teacher with integrated curriculum goals; children's interest a major criterion for topic selection.
Teacher plans in advance, presents topics, designs and prepares learning experiences.	Teacher observes children's investigation, uses student interest to determine next step of the project.
Teacher decides on objectives based on curriculum goals. Teacher may or may not include inquiry experiences and student research to achieve objectives.	Teacher webs to assess prior knowledge, then organizes project so students learn what they do not know; integrates curriculum objectives as project progresses; always involves child investigation.
Knowledge gained through teacher-planned experiences, resources brought into the classroom, small- and large-group activities, and events.	Knowledge gained by finding answers to questions or investigation; children involved in determining the activities and the events and how to find answers.
Resources are provided by the teacher but students may also bring in resources.	Resources are brought in by students, the teacher, and experts who visit the classroom or are gathered on field-site visits.
A field trip may or may not be included. If included, field trips may occur at any time but often near the end to culminate the study.	Field-site visits are an important part of the project process. Students may do several site visits in one project. Field-site visits usually occur early in project.
Topic often taught at specific teacher-determined times in the day, or it may be integrated into many content areas and permeate the day.	Project permeates the day and the classroom, involving many different curriculum areas and skills.
Activities (such as making a craft, doing a science activity) are planned by teacher to learn specific concepts.	Activities focus on investigation, finding answers to questions, using resources. Teacher assists integration of concepts during debriefing and discussion.
Representation relates to specific activities—drawing to show observations in a science experiment, creating maps, drawing a picture, writing a play. Representation activities aren't usually repeated.	Representation (drawing, writing, building, constructing) challenges children to integrate concepts. Representation documents what children are learning. Activities are repeated to show growth in knowledge and skills as project progresses.

able adult. The academic tasks in the early childhood curriculum usually address facts and skills that the majority of children are unlikely to learn spontaneously or by discovery, though, under favorable conditions, many children do so. For example, under the right environmental conditions, many young children can "pick up" the names of colors and shapes and need little in the way of didactic or systematic formal instruction to learn them. These items of knowledge may be spontaneously "constructed" by some children, as can be seen in invented spelling; but in such cases they are largely misconstructed and require assistance to reconstruct correctly.

Similarly, the alphabet, an arbitrary sequence of symbols developed over a long period of human history, has no inherent discoverable logic. It has to be mastered with the help of knowledgeable others who encourage frequent repetition and who correct errors until mastery is achieved. In the case of most young children, it would be wasteful and inefficient for them to have to "discover" such things as the alphabet, or punctuation rules, the pledge of allegiance, the national anthem, or other conventional knowledge by self-initiated discovery processes.

While academic goals address small units of knowledge and skills, intellectual goals address dispositions; that is, habits of mind that include a variety of tendencies to interpret experience (Katz, 1993). Some habits of mind that relate to intellectual goals include the disposition to

- Make sense of experience
- Theorize, analyze, hypothesize, and synthesize
- Predict and to check predictions
- Find things out
- Strive for accuracy
- Be empirical
- Grasp the consequences of actions
- Persist in seeking solutions to problems
- Speculate about cause-effect relationships
- Predict others' wishes and feelings

Along with many others not mentioned, these dispositions are all intellectual rather than academic in focus.

It is reasonable to assume that the most important intellectual dispositions are inborn in all humans and are likely to be fairly robust in very young children. For example, the dispositions to make sense of experience, to be curious, and to be empirical can be observed in virtually all very young children, regardless of family income and environment.

Intellectual dispositions deserve explicit attention in curriculum planning and teaching methods so they can be manifested, appreciated, and thereby further strengthened and developed. Unless the curriculum provides contexts in which the intellectual dispositions can be strengthened by being used and applied meaningfully, they may be weakened or even lost. If they are lost, they may be very difficult to reinstate. Margaret Donaldson (1978) noted that all children seem to begin their school experiences with eagerness to find things out and to pose questions, and to do what is asked of them in school. She also notes that "the problem then is to understand how something that begins so well can often end so badly" (p. 14).

Unfortunately, what happens in some classrooms promotes neither academic nor intellectual goals. Some children spend much time on relatively mindless activities like cutting and pasting pre-cut Valentine hearts, and in group discussions from which the majority of the participants withdraw psychologically within minutes. These involve limited academic skills and do not provide for the development of intellectual dispositions.

Such activities do not sufficiently challenge children to identify and solve problems but instead emphasize passive following of instructions or being entertained. These experiences are often justified on the basis of their being "fun." While such activities may not harm and may be beneficial in a few ways, they lack sufficient intellectual vitality to support or strengthen the intellectual dispositions.

Project Approach and the Larger Curriculum

Involving young children in project work is unlikely to offer all of the learning experiences that should be included in their curriculum. There are many other learning activities that are beneficial for the young child.

However, classrooms where children are actively engaged in projects are also classrooms where children sing, listen to stories, build block structures, paint, participate in dramatic play, and learn and practice emerging skills. Projects are compatible with many different curriculum approaches and classroom structures and environments. Units, thematic teaching, and direct instruction can provide good learning experiences for some skills and some topics. In many of the classrooms described in this book, units and projects were progressing at the same time. Projects are unlikely to constitute the whole child care, preschool, kindergarten, or first-grade curriculum.

Teachers who are comfortable with the project approach often very effectively incorporate features of the project process (such as construction, observational drawing, and documentation) into other types of learning experiences. Because of this, some units or thematic learning experiences look like projects. However, unless the elements of child initiation, child decision making, and child engagement are present in a learning experience, it is not a project, and it is less likely to provide the unique benefits of project work.

It is only when children are curious, absorbed, and interested in a topic that the benefits of projects are realized. Children benefit from the added opportunity to initiate, investigate, and follow through on their interests.

BENEFITS OF PROJECTS IN THE EARLY YEARS

Projects and Academic Achievement

With three of every five preschoolers now in childcare (Children's Defense Fund, 1998), a significant proportion of children's growing and learning time is spent outside the home. Many of these children are in group-care settings in which a large portion of the day is devoted to teacher-directed learning experiences. These experiences often do not provide opportunities to take initiative and responsibility for the work undertaken, as in the experiences of project work. A number of studies have documented the benefits of opportunities for children to direct their work, and to follow their interests by self-selection of activities and exploration of materials (Schweinhart, 1997).

> The relevant evidence from these studies suggests that preschool programs based on child-initiated learning activities contribute to children's short- and long-term academic and social development, while preschool programs based on teacher-directed lessons obtain a short-term advantage in children's academic development by sacrificing a long-term contribution to their social and emotional development. On this basis, research supports the use by preschool programs of a curriculum approach based on child-initiated learning activities rather than one based on teacher-directed lessons. (p. 2)

The benefits of children's having substantial control over the work undertaken extend beyond the early years. Marcon (1992, 1995) found that children from preschool classes that offered ample opportunity for child-initiated, as opposed to teacher-directed, activity showed the greatest mastery of basic reading, language, and mathematics skills. At fourth grade, children who had experienced self-initiated learning also had higher overall grade-point averages and also higher grade-point averages in most individual subject matter areas. Boys may especially fare better in school in the long run when they have experienced a preschool that emphasizes self-initiated learning (Marcon, 1992; Miller & Bizzell, 1983).

Too often schools and childcare centers, especially those with high concentrations of children from low-income families, compound the problem by limiting experiences to large-group instruction in isolated sub-skills and extensive drill and practice (Knapp, 1995). An opportunity to follow their interests, to acquire new interests, and to investigate a topic in depth can be highly beneficial for academic achievement of children in these environments. It can also assist social and emotional development.

Projects and Social and Emotional Development

Children of all socioeconomic backgrounds can benefit from emotional involvement in and commitment to finding things out and mastering new knowledge and skills. Missed opportunities to become meaningfully engaged in a topic of interest may affect the development of dispositions to achieve and learn. If a school or a childcare center neglects the provision of opportunities for emotional involvement in learning experiences,

children's inborn curiosity and desire to learn may not be sufficiently strengthened. Parents who have ample time and financial resources may provide these experiences for their own children within their family. They may watch for their children's emerging interests and then encourage them by buying books, taking trips, and providing resources for further knowledge about the topic. The parents model emotional involvement in learning for the child. Children who spend extended periods of time in group care may not have sufficient experience of this support of their individual interests.

Research suggests that there is a relationship between the role that children have in determining their own learning experiences and the development of social skills. A study of kindergarten classes using three different teaching approaches (direct instruction, a constructivist approach based on child-initiated activities, and an eclectic approach) found that the children from the constructivist class were more interpersonally interactive. They exhibited a greater number and variety of negotiation strategies and shared more experiences (Devries, Reese-Learned, & Morgan, 1991).

Considerable interest has focused recently on the concept of engaged learning. Engaged-learning experiences are defined by Jones, Valdez, Norakowski, and Rasmussen (1994) as learning experiences in which learners take responsibility for their own work, are self-regulated, and are able to define their own goals and evaluate their own accomplishments. When students are energized by their own work, their disposition to solve problems and to seek deeper understanding can be developed and strengthened.

It is this engaged learning that occurs in the project approach when children have the opportunity to initiate, investigate, and follow through on their interests. Because these activities are so similar to the investigative process of adults, we began to call young children doing these activities "young investigators." In this book, we use young investigators to refer to children aged 3 to 6, who are engaged in active investigation of a topic through the project approach, although they have not yet achieved verbal fluency or mastery of basic literacy skills.

Projects and Parent Involvement

Another potential benefit of the project approach for young children is the readiness and ease with which parents become involved and interested in the children's work. Parents' involvement in their children's education is significantly related to children's success in school (Henderson & Berla, 1994).

There are many ways in which parents can become involved in projects. Epstein (1995) has specified six types of parent involvement that are valuable and can have an impact on student success. Four of these six key types can occur through parent involvement in projects. These include volunteering, learning at home, communicating with the home, and collaborating with the community. Teachers who implement the project approach in preschool, kindergarten, and first grade frequently report how interested and involved parents become in the projects. When young investigators talk extensively and enthusiastically at home about the projects and what they are learning, the communication about school increases.

When teachers carefully document the young investigators' experiences and share what children are learning through their investigations, parents are often amazed and delighted to see the level of thinking revealed. It is common for parents to become so interested that they take children to field-sites outside of school hours, purchase books or materials that relate to the topic, or bring resources and materials from the home into the classroom. Parents often serve as visiting experts and enjoy answering young investigators' questions or assisting in the teaching of relevant skills during a project. Sometimes parents participate in the investigation and accompany young investigators to community sites, where they learn about the topic alongside their children. Most projects end with a culminating event that includes a display of children's work, which also involves parents. During these events parents frequently comment on their surprise at how much learning has occurred.

As parents observe projects develop, they see engaged learning experiences and observe techniques for fostering engaged learning in the home. For example, a parent accompanying a class on a field-site visit may observe how the teacher encourages young investigators to ask questions and how he draws the children's attention to observing and recording. The parent may see very young investigators draw, write, and photograph. These are skills that many parents may not be aware that young children can do. The parent will also see how the teacher listens carefully to children's comments and questions and responds to them respectfully.

OPPORTUNITIES AND CONSTRAINTS OF THE EARLY YEARS

Developmental Milestones

Projects are especially valuable for children in the early years because this is a period of rapid intellectual growth that can have important long-term consequences. Berk (1991) discusses the competencies of intellectual development that emerge in the age range 2 through 4. These include:

- representational activity (development of language, make-believe play, meaningful drawings, and understanding of spatial symbols such as photographs, simple maps, and models)
- taking the perspective of others in simplified, familiar situations and in everyday communication
- distinguishing animate beings from inanimate beings
- categorizing objects on the basis of common function and kind of thing, not just perceptual features
- classifying familiar objects hierarchically (p. 237).

These competencies continue to develop during kindergarten and first grade.

Competencies such as those above have been identified through observation and children's performance on cognitive tasks. Additional insight into intellectual development is now coming from recent experimental developments in the study of early cognition such as observing the activity of the brain during cognitive activity and growth, and computer-assisted models of the brain's development of networks of information during early learning. Although it is too early to draw many conclusions from this new research, Catherwood (1999), in a recent review of these new views of the young child's growth and development, came to the following conclusion:

> The current body of developmental research has helped to make it clear that by the time the child is three or four years of age, there has already developed an enormously complex and interlinked knowledge base about the world. The tasks for early years educators may be . . . the further articulation and application of that web of understanding . . . engaging the child in an effort to gain a more explicit and articulated awareness and control over that knowledge base and subsequently to facilitate links between this knowledge and verbal expression. . . . it can be said that experiences that support the child in making connections amongst domains of knowledge (e.g. as in "event-based" programmes in which children develop activities around conceptual themes) are likely to impact on and enhance the richness of neural networks in the child's brain. (p. 33)

There are many experiences in project work that are consistent with Catherwood's conclusion. These include the focus of projects on topics in which the child has some background knowledge and interest, the integration of many domains of learning, the opportunity and purpose for verbal communication that emerges in project work, the "events" of field-site visits and visits by experts, and the development of activities by children.

In addition to the rapid general cognitive growth, a variety of skills related to competence in literacy begin to emerge as well as an understanding of the importance and usefulness of numerical concepts and skills. Children begin to learn about scientific inquiry. In a class that provides opportunities for project work, these intellectual dispositions and academic skills can be applied in ways that are clearly useful in the eyes of young investigators.

Projects and Literacy Development

The prekindergarten, kindergarten, and first-grade years are recognized as key years for the development of communicative competence, including language and understanding of symbol systems (Machado, 1995). While in the past teachers were sometimes discouraged from introducing reading and paper-and-pencil activities into the prekindergarten, teachers are now strongly encouraged to a provide a literacy-rich environment in kindergarten as well as preschool classes (Whitmore & Goodman, 1995). Although whole-group, formal instruction in reading and writing is still difficult for children from 3 to 5 years of age, children begin to represent concepts and ideas through drawing and early writing.

Our experience of working with many teachers who implement the project approach suggests strongly that among its many advantages is how it appears to strengthen young children's motivation to master a wide variety of skills. This response to project work seems to be related to the children's sense of *purpose* for the work undertaken. For example, the purpose for their early efforts to read signs, pamphlets, or books is to find answers to the questions generated in Phase I of the project. The purpose of writing may be to send messages, or to record observations made during fieldwork, rather than just to please the teacher, complete an assignment, or finish a chore whose purpose may be obscure to them.

Young investigators are often highly motivated to show others what they have learned about a topic. Young investigators create play environments, block structures, buildings, and other products related to the project. Often children want to show what they know about a topic by writing about it. As children build block structures related to a topic (e.g., a barn, during an investigation of a local farm), they often write signs to identify the parts of their structure (e.g., hay loft). When they make a dramatic play environment such as a restaurant, they may make signs or other literacy items to make their play environment more realistic (e.g., menus or notices of opening hours).

During the first phase of a project when the teacher engages the children in developing a web of ideas surrounding the topic (see Chapter 2), the children give teachers their thoughts to record on the web, and many strive to read what has been written. As they create child-

size versions of adult environments for dramatic play such as a hospital, they also role-play the reading and writing. Young investigators often copy and save words about things in which they are interested. Even for preschool children, posting of lists of project words encourages the child to learn the words and to use reading and writing as tools. In a study of first-grade children doing projects and units, children were more involved in reading and research in the project than in the teacher-directed unit (Bryson, 1994). Teachers whose projects are described in this book have made similar reports.

Projects provide a purpose for representation. Pam Scranton describes the experience of one 3-year-old who was drawn into representation through interest in the project:

> For example, Jordan had no interest in the Fire Truck project, but on the Vet Project he became involved. I have a picture [see Figure 1.3] of Jordan bending down to talk to Ashley. Ashley is describing what she is doing. Jordan marched over to me and said, "Can I have a clipboard, teacher?" Then he drew a horse. He had never written or drawn anything before. That would never have happened if I told him to do it. I just love to see children do that, to be motivated and to learn from each other. He was so proud of it. It wasn't a wonderful drawing; but it was a wonderful drawing by a 3-year-old. It was the first time Jordan had ever even wanted to pick up a pencil.

That is what project work often does: It causes many children to want to represent their ideas and observa-

Figure 1.3 Jordan (3 years old) observes Ashley (4 years old) drawing. Encouraged by her modeling, he then requests a clipboard to do his own drawing. Learning from peers is characteristic of project work.

tions by putting them down on paper in writing and through drawing.

Projects and Problem Solving

Most projects involve a wide variety of types of problem solving. In teacher-directed instruction, opportunities to solve problems are often limited. When the problems to be solved are set mainly by the teacher, the children are not necessarily motivated to search for solutions. However, problem solving develops naturally in the project process. Young children are consistently challenged in project work to solve mathematical problems and do scientific thinking. They become aware of the function of number and quantity concepts. Projects create a reason to quantify information as they gather it and to represent quantities with numerals. Projects also provide reasons to classify and sort, to develop categories for things so that they can think about them. Children learn to use tools for investigation, to experiment and observe the results, and to make comparisons among objects. Projects provide a natural provocation for learning and using mathematical and scientific thinking.

In the first phase of a project the children generate a list of questions. They then discuss possible strategies by which to seek answers to those questions. Even figuring out how to find the answers to these questions becomes a problem as they search for resources and experts. Teachers encourage children's problem solving by asking additional questions such as "Who could answer that question for you?" and "Where could you find out about that?" Sometimes young investigators solve problems by direct, first-hand investigation. For example, a question like "What's inside a radio?" led to the problem of how to get the radio open so that they could see inside it.

Project work with young children often results in constructing models, drawing diagrams and charts, and creating playing environments. These activities are often rich with opportunity for young children to solve problems by using measurement, counting, and graphing. In the course of this problem solving, children become aware of many mathematical concepts such as shapes, area, distance, and volume. For example, designing a model hospital with a limited number of blocks and building a grocery store in their classroom while still having space for other activities are problems that require serious group consideration and consultation. Individual young investigators may also have their own problem-solving experience within a project. For example, a child may investigate many ways to make a cardboard tree stand up in a display before finding the best way. Problem solving changes as a project progresses and new problems arise.

GUIDING PROJECTS WITH YOUNG CHILDREN

Structure of the Project Approach

Teachers of young children who have not had an opportunity to observe others guide project work are often at a loss as to how to get a project started and then follow it through. The structure of the project approach, however, provides guidelines for the process. It may be helpful for teachers who have not observed a project in action to read the summary of the Vet Project, a project by 3-, 4-, and 5-year-old children with Pam Scranton (see Figure 1.4). This summary provides an overview of one project's progress.

Teachers are frequently awed and incredulous at the stories of problem solving and the examples of observational drawing and early literacy skills that are collected by teachers who document the progress of a project. They are afraid that they will not know how to recognize and take advantage of the opportunities for problem solving, literacy development, and social-emotional experiences that are so beneficial to the young child's development. Some teachers also fear that doing projects with children means relinquishing control of the educational program to the children or that their classrooms will become chaotic.

The structure of the project approach, as defined by Katz and Chard (1989), can be used to guide the process and to reduce many of these teacher concerns. The structure consists of three distinct phases (see Figure 1.5). During these phases the teacher evaluates the suitability of a topic, anticipates needed resources, plans field experiences, and identifies experts who can be brought into the classroom for interviews and demonstrations. Documentation throughout the project helps the teacher recognize opportunities for problem solving and the application of concepts and skills so that good learning opportunities are not missed.

The project approach provides a structure but not a prescription for learning experiences. There is a fine line between supporting children's investigation and teacher-directed inquiry; between supporting children's learning and taking over the learning experience. One of the most challenging tasks in teaching young children is to learn how to recognize that line and how to avoid crossing it. The structure of the project approach can help teachers learn to do this. In learning how to implement the project approach, the teacher learns how to support and not crush children's curiosity and natural dispositions to learn and yet still achieve curriculum goals. "Approach" can be defined as "a way or means of reaching something," "an entry" (*The American heritage dictionary*, 1992). The project approach can be an

Figure 1.4 The Vet Project.

A Project by 3-, 4-, and 5-Year-Old Children at Bright Beginnings, Woodford County
Special Education Association, Eureka, Illinois.

Length of Project: 8 weeks   *Teachers: Pam Scranton, Brenda Wiles*

Phase I

Beginning the Project

The Vet Project began when one of the children, during morning group time, cried because he had to leave his kitty at the vet's to be neutered. After talking through the experience as a group, the rest of the children couldn't let go of the subject and continued to talk about David's kitty the rest of the morning. The next day we talked about the possibility of going to a vet clinic, and the children began asking questions and predicting what we would see. Kati shouted: "You better start writing, Teacher!" We started making a list of what they knew about a vet clinic. I discovered that they had a limited "vet vocabulary." We decided to go to the library to choose some research materials.

Phase II

Developing the Project

After the trip to the library, the children began reading the vet books and had some discussions about what kinds of animals we would see at the vet's. Some of the children thought that we would see monkeys, zebras, cows, and pigs. We made our beginning web and prepared interview questions for the vet. On the actual field experience, the children were divided into two groups. Those children most interested and involved in the project were responsible for graphing certain aspects of the clinic, recording answers to their questions, and sketching parts of the clinic. The expert, Dr. Marge, took the children through a typical exam and the children manipulated lots of the vet tools. After we returned to the classroom, the children began to make plans to construct their own vet clinic. They used their field sketches and photographs taken on the field experience to construct it, using boxes and the various scrounge items that parents brought into the classroom. The small group of children building the clinic were very concerned with making the clinic look as close to the one they had visited as possible, and they had to solve problems in the construction of key pieces of the clinic. This same group also visited the high school art class where the art students encouraged them to model with clay and represent the animals they saw at the vet clinic.

Phase III

Concluding the Project

As the month of May approached, the dramatic play that had been so intense a few weeks earlier began to wane. I gathered the project group together, and they decided to take down the vet clinic. We made another web and found that they knew a lot more "vet words" now and could tell anyone the important parts in a vet clinic and why they were needed. We made a list of their ideas about sharing their learning with their parents and the ECE class next door. The group decided to make a book. They then made a list of important things they wanted included in the book. They collected the displayed drawings and graphs from the walls for processing into the vet book.

---

entry, a way for teachers to reach their goal of supporting active, engaged, meaningful learning and intellectual development. For some teachers, it can be an entrance into teaching in a more effective, child-responsive way. It is important to remember, however, that an entryway is never the end destination and that the structure of the project approach is a guide to supporting children's learning, not the end result.

Organization of This Book

As the structure of the project approach provides a guide for supporting children's projects, this book provides a guide for teachers to learn how to do projects. Chapters 2 to 5 explain the phases of the project approach in detail, focusing particularly on how these phases look in childcare and education programs for young children. Step-by-step explanations of the phases are accompanied by illustrations and children's work from actual projects. Chapter 5 also presents a variety of methods of documentation and a framework for evaluating the project and extending and expanding the approach in future projects. Chapter 6 addresses the issue of using the project approach to meet required curriculum goals or academic standards. It also addresses how early literacy experiences and other academic skills can be strengthened during project work. A number of other issues that teachers often want to discuss are also presented. These include involving parents, utilizing technology, and using the project approach with specific populations including children with special needs, second-language learners, and toddlers. The chapter also presents ways that administrators can support project work.

Figure 1.5 Phases of a project.

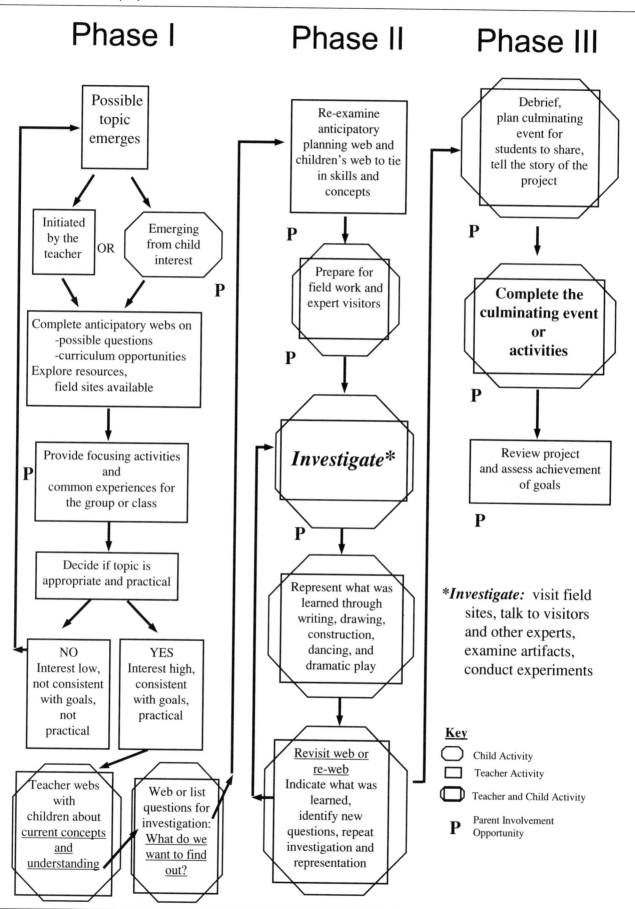

Phase I

Possible topic emerges

Initiated by the teacher OR **Emerging from child interest** P

Complete anticipatory webs on
-possible questions
-curriculum opportunities
Explore resources, field sites available

P **Provide focusing activities and common experiences for the group or class**

Decide if topic is appropriate and practical

NO Interest low, not consistent with goals, not practical

YES Interest high, consistent with goals, practical

Teacher webs with children about <u>current concepts and understanding</u>

Web or list questions for investigation: <u>What do we want to find out?</u>

Phase II

Re-examine anticipatory planning web and children's web to tie in skills and concepts
P

Prepare for field work and expert visitors
P

Investigate*
P

Represent what was learned through writing, drawing, construction, dancing, and dramatic play

<u>Revisit web or re-web</u>
Indicate what was learned, identify new questions, repeat investigation and representation

Phase III

Debrief, plan culminating event for students to share, tell the story of the project
P

Complete the culminating event or activities
P

Review project and assess achievement of goals
P

****Investigate:*** visit field sites, talk to visitors and other experts, examine artifacts, conduct experiments

<u>**Key**</u>

⬭ Child Activity

☐ Teacher Activity

▱ Teacher and Child Activity

P Parent Involvement Opportunity

Chapter 7 is a description of one project, the Fire Truck Project, which prompted the reflections Pam Scranton shared at the opening of this chapter. A timeline of this first project undertaken by this group of 3- and 4-year-olds, one with special needs, documents the project's progress from its beginning, with the surprise viewing of the fire truck, to the culminating event, the "movie party." Ms. Scranton's thoughts about the young investigators, what they learned and what she learned about doing projects with young children, are also included. (A companion video of the development of the Fire Truck Project is available from Teachers College Press.)

At the end of the book is the Project Planning Journal, which teachers may copy and use in guiding young investigators. Originally designed to support teachers doing their first project with young children, the journal became a preferred way to plan and organize for project work by many experienced teachers. It became, in subsequent projects, a journal in which the teachers could record the progress of the project and their thoughts, and note documentation that had been collected. This journal was used by teachers in a number of the projects described in this book. Readers will find references to specific parts of the journal as they read about the project approach in Chapters 2 to 7.

Using the journal, however, is not a requirement for undertaking the project approach. There is no workbook for doing a project with young children. The journal and projects in this book are offered to support teachers as they learn to follow the interests of their children in implementing the project approach. Although different groups of young children may be interested in similar topics and do similar project activities, the course of projects is never the same. Authentic projects such as these cannot and should not be duplicated.

Learning to do projects is a journey, a journey that we have been privileged to share with the teachers in this book. The journey appears to be never-ending and teachers of young investigators appear never to stop learning from children how they can do it better. The sharing of the journey begins in Chapter 2: Getting Started.

Getting Started

In Phase I of the project the topic is selected. The teacher evaluates the feasibility of the topic by looking at curriculum opportunities using a teacher-planning web. She also assesses the availability of resources, expert visitors, and field-sites. Focusing activities are planned that provide children with a common knowledge base to begin investigation. The phase ends with generation of a web of current concepts and understanding. This is followed by the young investigators' generating a list of questions for investigation. As the questions for investigation become clear, Phase I comes to a close and the project moves into Phase II, Investigation. The flowchart of Phase I presents graphically the progress of the project during the beginning (see Figure 2.1).

SELECTING PROJECT TOPICS

The most important components of Phase I are the process of selection of the project topic, how it is introduced to the children, and helping the young investigators formulate the questions that will be the essence of their investigation. There are a number of issues that deserve consideration when launching a project with young children. Once these factors have been addressed, the groundwork is laid for the second phase of the investigation.

Common Experiences

The nature of a topic for young children to investigate contributes substantially to the quality of the work that can be accomplished. Compared with older, elementary school children, preschoolers, kindergartners, and first graders have as yet accumulated less-varied experiences on which to draw. Because prior experiences may be of a limited variety, young investigators are also likely to have fewer experiences to which all the class members can relate. In general, teachers imple-menting the project approach with young children spend more time and effort providing common experiences and eliciting interest and curiosity than do teachers of older children.

When a group of young children is new to project work, the fact that they have common experiences related to the topic increases the chances that all of them can contribute questions, suggestions, and ideas for how the investigation might proceed and what it should include. We have worked with several kindergarten teachers who have started project work with a study of the children's school bus, primarily because in their particular schools every child traveled on one and thus could readily suggest many features of it to raise questions about and to examine more closely.

For some topics, the teacher helps to get a project launched by providing common experiences for the class. However, in such cases, because the teacher is making decisions about the first steps, there is a risk of making a project into another teacher-telling or teacher-directed experience. The central feature of a project, as we use the term, is that the children, in discussion and consultation with their teacher, take initiative, make decisions, and take major responsibility for what is accomplished. If the teacher overstructures the children's experiences, the project does not provide opportunities for kinds of development and learning that come from child-initiated activities.

Determining Children's Interests

Project topics are most likely to elicit good responses from young children when they are either already among their interests or something that can engage their interests fairly readily. Thus one of the teacher's tasks early in a project is to identify the young investigator's current and emerging interests as well as to consider what new interests they might just be ready to acquire. Teachers should not hesitate to encourage children to acquire new interests.

Figure 2.1 Flowchart of Phase I.

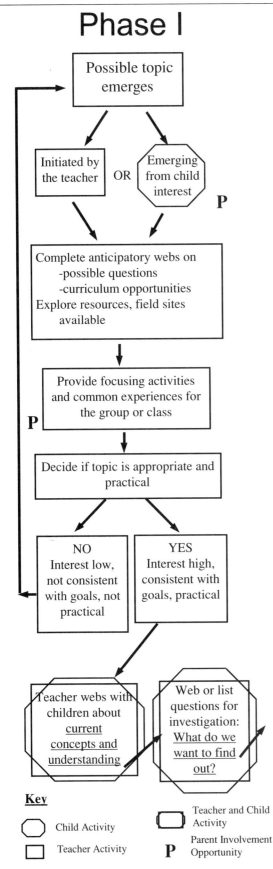

Phase I

Possible topic emerges

Initiated by the teacher   OR   Emerging from child interest   **P**

Complete anticipatory webs on
-possible questions
-curriculum opportunities
Explore resources, field sites available

P   Provide focusing activities and common experiences for the group or class

Decide if topic is appropriate and practical

NO
Interest low, not consistent with goals, not practical

YES
Interest high, consistent with goals, practical

Teacher webs with children about <u>current concepts and understanding</u>

Web or list questions for investigation: <u>What do we want to find out?</u>

Key

⬡ Child Activity

▭ Teacher Activity

⬭ Teacher and Child Activity

P Parent Involvement Opportunity

A few children may spontaneously express interest in a particular object (e.g., a backhoe being used outside the school for road repairs), an event (e.g., a classmate goes to the hospital), a particular place (e.g., a nearby restaurant) or a story or book about a topic. Young investigators may demonstrate this interest for the teacher by asking questions or requesting more information on the topic.

With younger children, many with limited verbal skills and vocabulary related to a topic, the teacher can look for expressions of interest through their behavior, perhaps by observing their spontaneous play. Three-year-olds will push forward for a closer view of an item that interests them. They often pick up items, or hoard "souvenirs" of experiences such as those collected on a class walk. The very young child also signals interest by extending the typical length of time focusing on objects or listening to conversations. Young investigators who are interested in a topic, even though very young, often attend closely to what other children say and think as well as listen to the teacher.

Child-Initiated Topics

Children often initiate their own projects. Sometimes the topic emerges out of an event that provokes the children's curiosity. Suddenly something happens and the class becomes immersed in a topic with intense interest and raises many questions for investigation. The event or experience that sparked the interest in a particular topic is called a *catalytic event*, something that causes a series of processes to begin. For example, building construction commonly becomes the focus of a project when construction of a building begins near the school or center and children observe it as they go to and from school or from the play-yard. One characteristic of a project that comes from a catalytic event is that it often moves into the investigation phase more quickly because the young investigators all have a common experience. The Fire Truck Project in Chapter 7 began with the catalytic event of seeing a fire truck during a walk.

In another school, a group of 4-year-olds became intensely interested in the experiences of a classmate who was anticipating a tonsillectomy. On learning of this impending event, the teacher made arrangements with the hospital for the class to have a guided tour especially designed for young children. The children's interest in the hospital grew and deepened into an extensive project that included exploring an ambulance brought to the school site and of which they prepared drawings to use as a basis for building one of their own in the class. They examined the emergency equipment, interviewed the drivers, and conducted an intensive investigation of many other related subtopics.

Teacher-Initiated Topics

A teacher may also choose a topic because it seems to provide beneficial experiences. For example, in the Car Project, which was documented by Sallee Beneke, Director of the Illinois Valley Early Childhood Education Center, in *Rearview Mirror* (1998), the car was considered as a topic because one child, Taylor, was interested in mechanical processes. He had, up to that time, not engaged in a variety of classroom activities or participated in previous projects. These teacher-initiated topics work best with young children if they are broad enough to allow for a wide range of possible interests among the children in the class. On the basis of her examination of the curriculum goals and on what she had learned from her extensive previous teaching experience, Ms. Beneke decided that it was a broad enough topic to be able to provide subtopics of potential interest to all of the children. However, she also knew that it is difficult to predict with certainty whether the children will respond with interest and enthusiasm to a given topic and waited for commitment to the topic until she observed the children's response to focusing activities.

An example of a teacher-initiated project is the Real Estate Project that occurred in Judy Cagle's multiage classroom. She initiated an investigation of the topic of houses when she discovered that a subdivision was under construction across from the school. She realized that the young investigators would have an opportunity to observe the development of the subdivision from the first digging to the actual sale of the houses over a period of the entire school year. As the project developed, she listened and watched for the young investigators' expression of interest as they progressed into the first phase of the project. Although they began with drawing the site and the earth-moving equipment, they became very interested in the real estate signs and the process of selling the houses. Gradually the project came to focus on the buying and selling aspects of the subdivision's development, and it became an investigation into the development of a real estate office.

Sometimes a project will grow from a teacher-initiated unit or theme. An example of this is the Apple Project at Hong Kong International School. The teacher, Mary Jane Elliott, typically begins school with a unit on apples. This unit led to the investigation of apples and the Apple Project. Although Ms. Elliott initiated the topic, the investigation of apples was the children's idea. Projects often grow out of planned units or themes in this way. The Art Museum, another project in Judy Cagle's classroom of 3- and 4-year-olds, grew from a unit on Eric Carle, the author of several favorite children's books.

General Guidelines for Selecting Topics

Even with extensive experience in implementing project work, teachers are often surprised by how young investigators respond to a topic: Some projects that they expect to work well fail to engage the children, and others they were skeptical about seem to take off. Furthermore, teachers have reported that topics that are embraced enthusiastically by a group of preschoolers one year have been rejected by those in the 4-year-old class another year.

Although it is clear that topics of interest to the children should be the main focus of a project, it is also important to note that not all interests of children are equally worthy of the kind of time and effort involved in good project work. Katz and Chard (1997) provided the following topic-selection guidelines for planning projects for children of any age.

1. The investigation should help children understand their own experience and environment more fully and accurately. However, not all phenomena in children's experiences and environments are equally worthy of their attention and energy.
2. The topic should strengthen children's disposition to look closely at phenomena in their environments worthy of appreciation.
3. The topic should provide ample opportunity to employ a wide variety of interactive skills and dispositions during the investigation.
4. The topic should provide opportunity to develop insight into the functions and limitations of a variety of different media and to develop skillfulness in applying the various media to their work.

Practical Considerations in Topic Selection

Along with the guidelines for topic selection for children of all ages, there are practical considerations for topic selection for projects with young children. These considerations respond to the nature of how the young child learns and the fact that young children have not yet mastered reading and writing. Since the success of a project with young children is so closely related to the appropriateness of a topic, the following topic criteria can be useful, especially for the first project undertakings.

1. *Projects are likely to be successful with young children when the topic is more concrete than abstract and involves an abundance of first-hand, direct experiences and real objects that young investigators can manipulate.* The ready availability of artifacts, objects, or items related to the project topic (e.g., a sling or stethoscope in a hospital project) enables young investigators to explore the phenomena in ways that are most effec-

tive for them: touching, moving, carrying, modeling, hearing, tasting, looking closely. When the topic itself is defined in concrete terms (such as the "Fire Truck" rather than "Fire Fighting" or "Fire Safety"), young children can more easily generate specific questions for investigation.

2. *Projects for young investigators are more successful if the topic is easily related to their prior experiences.* It is difficult for young investigators to think about topics for which they have little background experience or vocabulary. The topic "Boats" might be appropriate for young children who live around them and have some first-hand experience of them. Without such experience, the topic is unlikely to lead to children's taking initiative and productive effort without a great deal of teacher direction.

3. *Topics for which there are related sites nearby that can be conveniently visited enhance the project because young investigators are able to visit and revisit a number of times as the investigation proceeds.* Young children often have difficulty focusing on the topical issues when making a first site visit, and tend to benefit especially from returning to it with new questions. As they progress in the project, they also develop a better understanding of how to use observational skills and of what they want to accomplish in the project. Studying the lawnmower, which is used to mow the school lawn, might be a better topic than studying airplanes because the latter involves the complexities of a trip to the airport. When there is no possibility of revisiting a site, the teacher has to make plans to "capture the site" and bring it back for frequent revisiting—perhaps by means of videotaping the site visit and taking photos or slides of important items observed.

4. *Topics that enable young investigators to do research with minimal assistance from adults are more likely to lead to successful proje*cts. Investigations for young children consist of observing, manipulating, experimenting, asking questions, trying out ideas, and visiting places. Young investigators are less likely to become deeply involved in the work when their role is passive and receptive rather than active, and when they have to rely on secondary sources such as books, videos, encyclopedias, or experiences of adults. Thus historical topics are not likely to work well for projects for young children. "Pioneer Life" or "The Sinking of the *Titanic*" are not appropriate project topics for young children in that they necessarily require secondary sources of information. The study of "Pioneers," however, might be an appropriate project topic for older children who can read, use encyclopedias and the Internet, and understand media presentations and extended timelines.

5. *Projects are likely to be more productive with young investigators when they can represent what they know and learn by using skills and techniques appropriate for their age.* In the process of selecting a topic, teachers may find it helpful to think how information, concepts, and skills that have been learned can be represented in drawings, paintings, sculptures, or role-play events. It appears to be especially helpful for young investigators to become involved in creating large structures in which they can play. For example, the Fire Truck Project included building a fire truck out of a cardboard box. In principle, the younger the children involved in a project are, the more important it is that the topic has rich potential for dramatic play and construction. Mary Ann Gottlieb, kindergarten teacher, comments:

> I think the projects that allow us to either play in a dramatic sense or create a functional object or place, such as the bakery, have more interest. This stands to reason because the children are actively involved on a daily basis. In the Hospital Project we made a hospital in the hallway and it was a dramatic play situation for them. They were playing in that hospital. In the Bakery Project we actually made a bakery and sold baked goods, and in the Candle Project we actually made candles. This created a lot of interest.

6. *Projects that relate to the program's or district's curriculum goals are likely to be more easily supported by parents and administrators.* Many childcare centers and schools have specific curriculum guides that teachers are expected to follow. These guides designate objectives considered by the sponsoring agency to be worthy of learning. Curriculum guides can be a good source of broad topics for exploration. For example, a kindergarten teacher with the science objective "to understand what living things need to survive" might begin a search for a topic by exploring children's prior knowledge about plants or animals. Curriculum goals, especially those that relate to early literacy skills, emergent writing, number awareness, and scientific investigation, can be integrated into projects that are totally student-initiated. In fact, projects present many opportunities for young investigators to see the value of those skills and to apply and practice them in an authentic context. Mary Ann Gottlieb explains:

> Required curriculum fits naturally into projects. For example, take math, when you need to measure you measure! In a previous project, the children learned to measure. Today when we were reading a story about an elephant, it

told how big the elephant was. I had a little girl jump up and get a ruler to measure how long an elephant's trunk would be. She learned to do that in projects. Depending on what your topic might be, you can use objects for sorting, classifying, and patterning. Any construction you make involves mathematics and you as a teacher find that you can pull the math in when it is relevant—number recognition, one-to-one correspondence, measuring.

7. *Projects are more likely to lead to in-depth learning and transfer of skills if they are on topics that are culturally relevant to the children and their families.* The world of young children is relatively confined with a major portion of it consisting of the family and their immediate environments: the home, the neighborhood, and the school or center. Topics about these environments are more likely to capture children's interest because they have some prior knowledge. They are more likely to be interested in the pick-up truck that Daddy drives than the airplane they have never seen. If children are to become actively engaged, the topic must be a topic with which they have some familiarity.

Young children in Peoria, Illinois, seem particularly interested in construction equipment. One reason may be that many Peoria-area parents or neighbors are employed by Caterpillar, Inc., or Komatsu-Dresser, companies that build tractors, engines, trucks, and other products used in the heavy construction industry. As the children observe these massive machines in road building or on work sites, their parents point them out and discuss them. Interest in construction equipment is part of the culture of the central Illinois area and a popular project topic.

When the topic has local relevance, interactions between parents and children are more likely to occur. Parents then reinforce what is being learned in the center or school and can support the dispositions to be curious and to find answers and solutions to the issues being investigated. In other words, parents can contribute significantly to a project if it is also relevant for them.

Reflecting on these practical considerations outlined above when selecting a project topic increases the chances that teachers will identify topics that have the greatest probability of success with young children and at the same time contribute to meeting their curriculum requirements.

Reports of Successful Topics

Because the success of a project depends on the prior knowledge, environment, interest, and curiosity of the children, the development of a list of recommended topics for young children is difficult. As discussed above, the issues in topic selection are so complex and the importance of children's interests and curiosity so vital that such a list might actually do more harm than good. Barb Gallick describes some of the projects that have been successful in her childcare program for a group of mixed age 3- through 5-year-olds.

> During fall semester we did two projects: the butterfly garden and building a tree house. Both were based on events that occurred to the children in our center, and we scaffolded these into project topics.
>
> We also began a project last spring on vehicles/forms of transportation, which the children turned into a project on a Monster Truck Parade. The children planned a parade from beginning to completion using monster truck toys they brought from home—other entries were allowed! This turned out quite well also. . . . So far this semester we have yet to find a common theme among our children's play or discussions. We are watching carefully, but two topic ideas that the teachers are tossing around are the pet store or pets and the post office.

It is just as difficult to classify inappropriate topics as appropriate topics. Although space travel might not at first seem like an appropriate topic, if the classroom were near a shuttle launch area, it might be very appropriate, especially if many of the children's parents were employed in the space industry. In the process of selecting topics, there is no substitute for being a good listener and knowing your children, their families, their culture, and their interests.

Divergent Interests

In a class or group of children, the range of interests is likely to be very wide, adding one more challenge to the selection of project topics. Furthermore, the chances of all members of the group being equally interested in a given topic are very small. It is to be expected that some young investigators will participate and respond more eagerly to one topic than to another. Projects are occurring alongside many other activities in the classroom such as block building, stories, dramatic play, and so forth. Young investigators will approach each project in different ways. Pam Scranton describes the approach of her 3-year-olds:

> We may have some children who are not interested in a topic. I have learned that children, especially the 3-year-olds, might be drawn into

the project later or they might not at all. They may be very involved, however, in the next project.

Even though some children may not contribute to the investigations, they are often interested in reports of the work others are doing and may learn much about the topic by observing them as they build structures and discuss the progress of their project plans.

Teachers who are new to the project approach and work with multi-age groups sometimes think that the range of abilities and experiences of the children adds additional challenges to implementing project work. However, the combination of ages in the group enhances project work by providing contexts in which older children can initiate the complex activities in which younger ones participate but could not have initiated by themselves. Older children can take the initiative in the investigation, and the teacher can encourage them to find appropriate roles for the younger ones and strengthen their own growing competencies by teaching what they are learning. Older children can provide many verbal and fine motor skills the younger ones are only just beginning to develop. In the case of mixed-age groups, the process of selecting project topics should include consideration of the different ways that children in the age range can become interested and involved in the topic.

Some teachers are concerned that children with special needs or developmental delays may not be able to participate in projects. However, teachers of these children typically report that if they readily show marked interest in a particular topic, they easily become engaged in project work. The teacher can make appropriate adaptations to ease their involvement in project work in the same way that she does so for other classroom work for such children. This is discussed more fully in Chapter 6.

A special challenge for teachers of preschool and kindergarten children is that many are working in half-day or alternate-day class sessions. This can be particularly challenging if teachers have more than one class in their classroom within a day. Teachers new to projects are often concerned that different topics would emerge from each group of children, putting the classroom and the teacher in the predicament of providing resources, work space, and planning for two or more different project topics. Teachers who have two classes of children have found that projects can be successful by using a broad topic for all groups. By recording the young investigators' comments in developing the webs and lists of questions, the teacher looks for common interests and questions. The classes can share responsibility for conducting the investigations and finding the answers. When the projects move into construction, then two classes can share responsibilities for particular parts

of the construction. For example, in building a grocery store, one class constructed the checkout area and another, the meat department. Each group followed its own investigation of the subtopics.

Although finding a topic that would be meaningful to two separate classes seems like a difficult challenge, it often works out quite well. In one case, a morning kindergarten class was more interested than the afternoon class in a specific topic. The afternoon class agreed to participate in the investigation of the topic selected with the understanding that the next time they would choose the project topic. As it turned out, as the investigation progressed, both classes found subtopics that interested them, and the topic worked well for both sessions.

Teachers can also take advantage of the opportunity that arises from these challenges to teach and support communication skills. Several kinds of learning can be fostered by asking children of one group, perhaps the morning group, to dictate or draw messages for the afternoon group about what they are planning, and to solicit ideas from them. A teacher of a morning and afternoon group of 4-year-olds found that when she debriefed the groups at the end of their sessions and asked them to dictate or draw such messages for the other group they were thoughtful, respectful, and encouraging of each other's efforts. In this way they learned quickly to offer supportive suggestions. The young investigators had opportunities to use in a purposeful way the kinds of communicative and social skills that are useful throughout life.

Many preschool teachers have one group of children 3 days a week and another group on the other 2 days. This creates an additional dilemma for selection of a topic or for even doing projects at all. Sallee Beneke at the Early Childhood Center at Illinois Valley Community College has children who come part-time according to their parent's class schedule. Contrary to projects' being more difficult or impossible in this environment, Ms. Beneke (1998) has the following comment.

> My view is that with this pattern of attendance, it is actually to the preschool teacher's advantage to engage in project work as opposed to short thematic units. Project work provides a tie that binds the group together. It provides continuity and coherence in a situation where children's experiences do not flow on a day-to-day basis as they might in a child care center setting where all attend full time. Children who had not been at our center for several days would arrive expecting to pitch right in on the continuing development of the car. (p. 19)

The consideration of a topic that would appeal to a large number of children would appear to be especially important in a program with this type of schedule.

There are two final cautions about topic selection. Teachers would be wise to avoid selecting a topic of intense interest to only one or two young investigators in a class. This often occurs with young children who have a particularly keen interest in something very specific with which others in the class have little or no experience. Although it is certainly appropriate to encourage some of those specific or unique interests in other ways, a topic should be of interest to a majority of children in a class if it is to be the basis for a meaningful project. However, the teacher of young children should not think that all children in the classroom must be highly motivated by a particular topic before the project can begin.

The last caution is to avoid being drawn into multiple topics in one classroom of children who are beginning projects. It is very difficult to support simultaneously several meaningful projects at this age level unless the teacher has had extensive experience managing projects and the children are accustomed to project work.

ANTICIPATORY TEACHER PLANNING

Once a student-initiated or teacher-initiated topic has been identified, teachers can continue the planning process by "trying out" the topic. One way to do this is to make an anticipatory teacher-planning web. This web helps a teacher think about the ways that a project might develop. A web may have a central topic focus and a variety of mini- or subtopics branching off of it. Some kindergarten and first-grade teachers like to do teacher planning webs by taking required content or curriculum objectives and thinking about how that topic might support growth and progress in each area (see Figure 2.2). Other teachers prefer to develop a teacher-planning web by focusing on the concepts inherent in the topic (see Figure 2.3). Still other teachers anticipate what the children might ask. (see Figure 2.4). Some teachers put their thoughts on small Post-it® notes and arrange them several different ways, for example as a topic web, as a curriculum web, and as children's anticipated questions.

Inspecting these webs and reviewing the guidelines for selection of a topic earlier in this chapter can help a teacher assess the potential benefits of a topic. Once a topic is selected and the project moves into investigation, these webs can help a teacher predict directions in which the project might go and thus become prepared

Figure 2.2 Anticipatory teacher-planning web with curriculum concepts (from Parker Early Education Center staff).

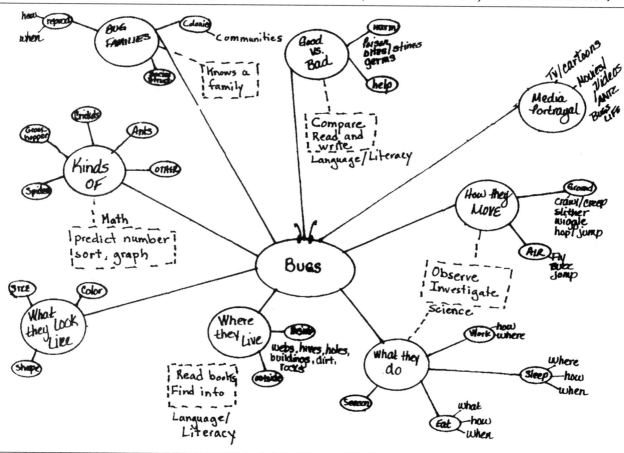

Figure 2.3 Anticipatory planning web with concepts about a topic (from Little Friends Learning Center staff).

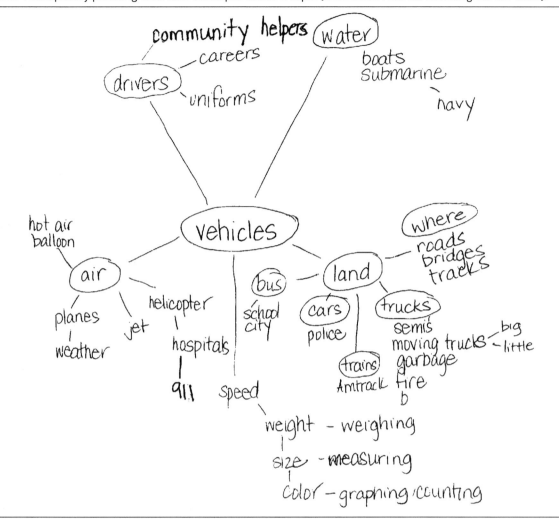

for lines of questions and suggestions from the children. Ideas for possible integration and application of knowledge and skills also emerge from this anticipatory webbing. Although it is a lengthy process, "trying out the topic" and making anticipatory planning webs not only assist a teacher in evaluating the worthiness and practicality of a topic, but also help a teacher to integrate components of a curriculum.

During this anticipatory planning process of webbing and reflecting on required curriculum, questions related to planning begin to emerge, for example:

- Are there experts that might be available to interact with the children?
- Are there sites that might be visited?
- How might parents respond to the topic?
- How might parents participate in the project?
- How might young investigators represent the findings of their investigation and the learning that results from it?

The answers to these questions help the teacher assess the viability of the topic as a project. In addition, the teacher can use the planning web to help identify resources, such as books, that the teacher may want to bring into the classroom to focus and enrich preliminary conversations and build common experiences.

BUILDING COMMON EXPERIENCES

If a topic is teacher-initiated, the teacher can use several strategies to provide a common background of experience for the young investigators so as to enrich their discussions and interactions before investigation begins. A teacher can tell a story of her own experiences and solicit similar stories from the children. An artifact, such as a piece of familiar equipment, might be shown to the children at group meeting time to provoke curiosity and discussion. A picture book can be read and

Figure 2.4 Anticipatory planning web with questions that children might ask.

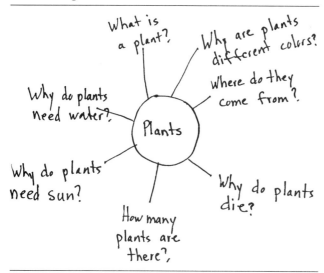

discussed. Conversations between children about the topic can be encouraged.

Because young children can represent their experience and understanding through their spontaneous play, teachers can begin a project by introducing props and costumes into a housekeeping or dramatic play area. As they use the artifacts in role-play, the young investigators represent and consolidate their understanding, and often exchange views related to the topic. Young investigators may also draw or paint what they know about a topic or build a block structure. It is important to build a shared perspective, a sense that a community is joined together to explore something of interest. Sharing and discussing these early explorations related to the topic help to build that shared perspective.

Pam Scranton describes her approach to the beginning of the Vet Project:

> The Vet Project is a good example of a project in which children had a limited knowledge base. David came in upset because his kitty had to stay overnight at the vet's to get spayed. He was very interested in finding out about this, but other children didn't know what a veterinarian was. My children had limited experience with this topic, but I thought the topic had promise for being a good project. So we spent several days just getting to know about the topic. We went to the library and the librarian had a few books about vets. She also had a computer game, "I Want to be a Veterinarian," where they were able to see the animal hospital on the screen. We just let them explore the library. Back in our classroom we

started reading the vet books. There were books about large animal vets, small animal vets, terms, etc. We were just collecting information and building a knowledge base.

These types of activities are sometimes called "messing around with the topic." They build background knowledge, establish some basic vocabulary, and introduce some concepts about the topic. This provides a critical knowledge base for the young investigator to draw on and is most important for the very young child. This period of time also enables the teacher to observe the children's interest in the topic.

FINDING OUT WHAT CHILDREN KNOW

Once the teacher determines that most of the children have developed some background on the topic, the teacher can find out what the children know about it in a more formal way. The teacher talks with the children and makes a graphic representation, such as a web, of what the children know. Graphic representations also contribute to the common knowledge base enabling discussion and assisting young investigators in developing familiarity with the vocabulary of the topic. Everyone involved—the teacher, the children, and even their parents—becomes aware of the children's beginning knowledge of the topic.

Lists

There are many ways the young investigator's knowledge can be recorded or represented. The simplest way to make a list of what the children know about the topic is by conducting a class discussion. Even this level of response requires considerable help from the teacher for most 3-year-olds. When the teacher writes the comments that children make on chart paper, they see the written equivalent of their words and concepts.

Webs

Webs are graphic representations of the relationships between the children's comments or questions. Webs are similar to lists except that the items are represented as radiating from a central idea. Sometimes teachers who are new to projects are hesitant to use webs because they think that young children can't read words and don't understand the relationships represented by the connecting lines. However, experienced project teachers report that young children seem to understand and respond to webs more readily than to lists. The process of having their words written down appears to be understandable to many 3-year-olds. Adding drawings or photos to the web assists the youngest children in connecting the written representation with their words and the words of the other children. Many 4-year-olds are actually able to explain the relationships between words when the teacher connects them on the web and are also often able to recognize the words. The key to success in making webs with young investigators is in the preparation and support given to the children during the first webbing experience and the care taken to be sure that children have enough prior knowledge of the topic to relate to the web in meaningful ways. Pam Scranton describes how she approaches webbing and listing with her mixed-age 3- and 4-year-old class where children with special needs are included.

> I feel that they have to be thinking about the topic quite a bit before we stare at that big blank piece of paper and start to web. Before we web, we always discuss the topic at least a couple of times. I will talk with children individually. I will even have a group discussion and ask questions such as "Where do you think we might want to go?" or "What might you want to see?"
>
> I web with a small group of about 8 of those children most interested in the topic. I have never been able to web effectively with the whole class together. . . . I just use a big piece of paper, clip it to the easel and they just take off. Children grow in their ability to web. On the Fire Truck Project we had arrows going everywhere. With the same group in the Vet Project that followed the Fire Truck Project, they classified the web according to large and small animals. They initiated it and told me where to write. They listed the large and small animals on the two sides of the list. "Well you better put that on the large animal side," said one of them! [See Figure 2.5].
>
> If they are younger or have never done projects before, you have to lead them a little bit—model for them. It is very easy for them to get off track telling stories. That is one reason that we have lots of discussions to provide opportunities to enjoy these earlier before we web. I ask them things like "What do you want to know about the vet?" "What's the thing you want to know about the most?"
>
> In the Vet Project, I pulled out the books, and we looked at them again. That jogs their memory and reminds them of vocabulary. When looking at a picture of the operating room, one might ask "What do you want to know about in there?" Sometimes they just give me lists. Then they will get into questions. This is where I want them to go—to formulate questions for investigation. Sometimes the questions will just flow from the

Figure 2.5 When the children in Pam Scranton's classroom were working on the Vet Project, the children decided that their list should be divided into large and small animals.

Small Animals

"How come kitties got to get spaded?"

"Do doggies got to get shots like kids do?"

"Do they cry when they get a shot?"

"Do you take care of squirrels? They're little."

"How do you give medicine to doggies?"

Large Animals

"How do you reach a horse to give it shots?"

"How come horseys got to stand up all day?"

"Can you give sheep their haircut? You know, take their wool off?"

"How come cows go to the vet? Do they get sick too?"

web and I will put up another paper for listing questions or I may do another web of what we want to know about. In the Vet Project, the questions flowed right from the web of what we wanted to know. "Will there be pills there?" "Why do the dogs have to be in cages?" "What happens if a squirrel gets sick?"

Most of the teachers with considerable project experience report a significant difference between the first webs of children and their subsequent webs on later projects. Where young investigators are in a mixed-age group, the younger children appear to grasp the skill quickly from the more experienced children. It also appears that 3-year-olds who do not actually contribute to building a web also learn how to web. Teachers report that these same children may spontaneously contribute to webbing on the next project, sometimes even taking the lead. The key to webbing with young children appears to be spending enough time accessing prior knowledge and helping children build a vocabulary for thinking about and interacting about the topic.

Sometimes teachers have difficulty keeping children's attention during a webbing process. This is especially a challenge when children are not yet reading. It is important to remember that the primary purpose of webbing is to get children's ideas and questions into writing. Although it is helpful for children to sound out their own words and watch the teacher model the writing process, this can be done at many other times during the day. During webbing for projects, the teacher wants to keep the pace brisk and keep children's ideas coming quickly. If they have to wait too long to offer their contribution, they sometimes forget. It is also helpful to do a web on an overhead projector. The smaller space enables the teacher to write quickly and children can still see the writing process and follow it. Children can also point on the screen where they want the word to appear as the teacher writes it. Young children also enjoy the use of Post-it® notes for webbing if they get to place their note on the web.

Webbing with kindergarten and first-grade children is easier than with prekindergarten children, especially if they have had prior experience doing projects. These children are more able to focus on questions and to see relationships between concepts. Many of them enjoy thinking about how parts of topics are connected. The accessing of prior knowledge and extensive discussion before beginning webbing is not so vital to the outcome of the webbing as it is with the younger, less experienced children. For many kindergarten and first-grade children, putting a paper on the easel and asking for a list of questions will result in a good list of questions if the topic is appropriate and familiar to that group of children. The teacher can stretch the children's understanding of the topic and relationships between the subtopics in the way she organizes the webbing event. Mary Ann Gottlieb reports how she experimented with her mixed age 4- and 5-year-old class:

> I tried something different this year. In the past I would web by putting the ideas up, and I would do the organizing—deciding where to write or how to connect the ideas, myself. Now I want them to see the connections between things on their own. As children gave me their ideas, I put one idea each on a Post-it® note. We then came back later, sometimes the next day, and the children organized these notes into a web. I also am trying webbing by writing the ideas radiating like sun rays around a circle containing the topic. Then I have the children come back at a later time and organize them. I am seeing that they can do it. They find the commonalities between the ideas, and group these together. Then they figure out what we can call that. We just have to work at it piece by piece.

Ms. Gottlieb also has found it helpful to keep these webs. She copies them into a web book, which is made of 12" × 18" pages that she places in spiral binder. The book of webs is a history of their explorations over the year. They can go back to, add to, or revise, recall, and discuss what they knew and how much they learned.

Dramatic Play

As we have already suggested, young investigators often show what they know through their play. A teacher may provide props that relate to a topic in a family living or play area. As children represent roles using the props, they show their depth of understanding about the topic as well as their understanding of the roles of adults regarding the topic. Often teachers of young children use props in a play area as a focusing device, and then watch to see what is revealed about children's prior knowledge.

An example of this strategy is the introduction of menus, order pads, napkins, placemats, and aprons into the housekeeping area in anticipation of a project on restaurants. As children choose to use the items, they show not only what they know about restaurants but also their interest in the topic. This is an especially effective technique to use with children who are not yet very verbal or who are learning a second language or for children with special needs who have language delays. The teacher can extend the opportunity for children to show what they know by participating in the playgroup. In this way, objects can be requested by name, and the teacher can hand specific items to children to see how they use the item and what vocabulary they have already mastered. This can all be done as part of the role-play activities.

Drawings

Asking children to draw what they remember about an event or a favorite part of their experiences related to a topic is often used with older children at this stage of project work and can work quite well with some kindergarteners and most first-graders. Most children of preschool age find it more difficult to do this. Young investigators who have been involved in multiple projects, however, are more likely to be able to do this, and their drawings will help focus their thoughts and provide insight for the teacher into their concepts about the topic. For example, a drawing of a turtle may consist of a circle with a small circle for a head and a smile on the face. The teacher can see that the child has very little understanding of what a turtle's face might look like, how the mouth would function, or where the eyes are located.

Constructions

Young investigators also represent what they know through constructions. Often children will show their interest and also their beginning knowledge through spontaneously built block structures. For example, a small group of children consistently made construction sites in the block area and made blocks function as ground-moving equipment. These explorations can be encouraged by adding props related to the topic to the block area and also to the table toy area where Legos or other construction materials are available. The art area is another area where structures may develop that provide insight into the children's knowledge of a topic.

Preserving First Representations

The first representations constitute the beginning documents from which to build a full documentation of a project. As young investigators explore a topic, they produce evidence of their knowledge, skills, and dispositions related to the topic. These should be carefully preserved because they can become excellent sources of documentation of their experiences from which their growth can be inferred. All of the webs, structures, drawings, and play experiences at this preliminary stage of the project will provide vital sources of evidence of the growth that has occurred in the project when later webs, structures, drawings, and play experiences are collected. That is why it is important for teachers to label and date the products of children's work. Documentation is discussed in greater detail in Chapter 5.

DEVELOPING QUESTIONS
FOR INVESTIGATION

As the teacher documents beginning knowledge about the topic, she will also begin to get an idea of what the young investigators don't know and what they would like to know. With older 4-year-olds and 5- to 6-year-olds, questions often come quickly and naturally, and the teacher begins a list of questions that serves as the bases of the investigation. With younger children, however, asking what the child would want to know often results in the telling of a story instead. As Pam Scranton described above, the teacher can help the youngest investigators develop questions by carefully tuning in to a child's interest and framing some of the children's thoughts into questions.

"Is that something you would like to know about?"
"Would you like to know how to use that?"
"I am wondering about . . . ? What do you think?"

Sometimes the teacher may deliberately provoke thought by introducing an artifact and discussing it with the children.

"What do you suppose this is for?"
"How do you think this might fit with this?"

It is usually easier to stimulate the formulation of the research questions by asking the young investigators what they would like to know more about, or find out about. For example, in anticipation of the visit of an expert, the teacher can more easily get the children to generate a list of questions by asking them what they would like her to talk about, tell them about, say more about, show them, than by asking them, "What questions do you have?"

It is important to view the first list of questions as a beginning for the investigation process. The list may be replaced with an entirely new list as a new facet of the topic captures interest and may dwindle as answers are found.

SETTING UP THE CLASSROOM
FOR INVESTIGATION

Most prekindergarten and kindergarten classrooms have a block area, an art area with easels, a family living or dramatic play corner, a meeting area, and equipment for sensory and science exploration such as sand, water, or light tables. All of these are natural locations for project work. First-grade classrooms vary greatly in the amount of available space. For all age levels, a table or several shelves can be set aside to display artifacts, books, and other resources about the topic. Bulletin board space can be used to display webs, ongoing project word lists, photographs, and children's work. Since projects at the preschool and kindergarten level often result in some type of construction, it is helpful to have a large space where the project can be left undisturbed when other activities are occurring in the classroom. This encourages young investigators to come back and reflect on their work and add more detail.

Sometimes teachers replace an established area of the room with the project construction. For example, the block area can become the farm, and the family living area can become the restaurant. Deciding where to build a construction and how to make room for it in the classroom is part of the problem-solving process, and children can participate by contributing ideas and selecting a solution. Sometimes a hallway or common space such as a multipurpose room can be used for projects. Some projects result in a number of smaller constructions like clay sculptures. These can be stored in large plastic boxes with lids. These boxes for temporary storage are also helpful when there are two groups of children sharing the same room.

Gathering Equipment and Supplies

Some materials and equipment are especially useful when doing projects with young children regardless of the topic selected. These include construction materials, art materials, and literacy-related materials. Even though most preschool children are not yet reading, books are an important resource for projects. Picture books related to the topics are helpful, but books for older school-age children can also be informative if they have photos, drawings, or diagrams. Realistic books are better than fantasy books for projects with young investigators. Fantasy books (such as *The Very Hungry Caterpillar*, Carle, 1984) can provide the misinformation and are better saved for enjoyment at the end of the project.

In addition, there are some materials that all children in the group should have when they work on projects. Clipboards with pencils attached often become prized possessions of young investigators. Because clipboards are normally used by adults and not children, they signal to the children the importance of the project work. For young investigators, pencils are often attached by string and then stuck under the clip when carrying the board. A laundry basket or other large tote with handles is convenient for stacking clipboards and transporting them to the field-site. Individual journals are also helpful for writing and sketching about a project topic or classroom experiences. As constructions develop, individual children may become "experts" or "researchers" on a particular aspect of the project. For example, during the Fire Truck Project, Jordan became the "ladder person" and spent several days studying and constructing ladders. Individual storage space for a child's particular exploration of a topic encourages the child to come back to the project the next day and perfect his work.

Projects and the Daily Schedule

There are several approaches to doing projects in early childhood classrooms. Young children seem to benefit most from a schedule that is not segmented into short, discrete content areas, such as math time or reading time. Most early childhood teachers try to organize their day so that events flow smoothly and don't require abrupt shifts from one activity to another. A common way to arrange the schedule is to divide the day into blocks of time. It is important that children have at least 45 to 60 minutes for investigation and discovery. This time may be called choice time, free playtime, work time, or center time. Many early childhood classrooms use time blocks similar to the one in Figure 2.6. This chart shows time blocks throughout the day, typical activities that occur within those time blocks, and how the project can be integrated into the class day without changing the schedule. Project activities may occur in only one or two of these time blocks or in many time blocks on any particular day.

Children Take Charge

Sometimes during the exploration of the topic, a project will take on a life of its own. Sometimes a topic is of high interest to the children and unanticipated events occur that enable children to take charge and move the project. This is the story of Natalya Fehr and her first project with 4- and 5-year-olds at Little Friends Learning Center. The class had been exploring the topic of vehicles. They explored transportation vehicles (cars, buses) and emergency vehicles, and then began to focus on heavy equipment such as trucks, combines, backhoe loaders, bulldozers, and cranes.

I tried to focus their minds towards a choice for a topic. They turned me a different way. One of the children said, "My dad works at Caterpillar so why don't we make his big machines?" Another child said, "I have special tools and my dad has a special T-shirt with the symbol of the company on it. What if I give this T-shirt to you and you will be our boss?" I realized that the children were leading me to a topic. I stopped talking, and they started talking about people who worked at Caterpillar. While I was talking I could see the children fidgeting with excitement and their eyes sparkling. They agreed together that they would like to be workers and I could be their boss. Then one child said, "We have to have special rules for our work!" Then it was time for recess.

While we were outdoors we saw construction going on a short distance away and the children asked me if we could go closer. They were paying close attention to the tracks that the machine made in the dirt. They also pointed out the waist belts for tools that the workers wore and how they worked using their tools.

All of a sudden a big heavy machine came from behind a building and stopped between two houses. Right away he [the driver] proceeded to use the machine and dig. This was a perfect demonstration for the children. The children exclaimed, "It's a backhoe loader, a backhoe loader!" We watched this machine for about twenty minutes. . . . The children noticed a lot of details about this piece of equipment. The one child said, "What if we make this backhoe loader?" Another child said, "Let's draw a picture of it!"

Suddenly everything was out of my control and the children were motivated as a team to start this project. I quickly went inside and the children followed. They directed me to bring out paper and markers. I thought to myself, this is how a project

Figure 2.6 Scheduled time blocks and project activities.

Typical Time Blocks	Project Activities That May Occur at This Time
Greetings Gathering Time	Viewing of displays on tables regarding topic Browsing of books/resources on rug Reviewing and discussion of photos of previous work
Circle or Meeting Time	Exploration and discussion of new topics Sharing of group investigations Review of work Introduction of resources such as books, new artifacts Presentations by visiting experts
Work (or Center) Time (not less than 45 minutes)	Investigations by individuals or groups Meetings of small groups Opportunities for representation such as drawing, painting, working with clay Creating play environments Construction and building of models
Review Time	Reports by groups of progress Introduction of new ideas Sharing of representations Developing questions for further investigation
Outdoor Time	Project investigations and observations if relevant to topic Role-play related to project
Small-group Activities	Focusing of small groups on project work Demonstration or practice of related content or skills Continuation of work begun in work time Adults sharing resources in small groups Presentations or demonstrations by experts Project activities needing more teacher guidance (detailed construction, modeling, reviewing and discussing with groups)
Story or Book Time	Sharing of expository books on project topic Sharing of project history books Sharing of storybooks that relate to the topic and are realistic Journal writing
Music Time	Sharing of music related to the topic
Language/Literacy or Math Workshop Times (First grade)	Introduction of content skills useful for project work such as graphing, charting, counting, measuring, problem solving, reviewing and adding to the word wall, making items for communication needs of project (signs, invitations, brochures, thank you notes), writing in journals, writing narratives for displays and project history books

starts. We went outside again. They worked on their drawings. One of the children said, "Can we draw a plan of who will do which things?"

Each child was suggesting something and I didn't have time to write all their words exactly. But I tried to get down on paper everything they said! One child said "What will we name our team?" Another child said, "Yellow, Yellow" because this was the color of the backhoe loader. Another child said "Well, the machine has symbols on it and what if we use these also to name our team?" They decided between each other who would write the name. I helped David to spell the first part of *yellow* and then he had some problems, so Jessica helped to finish it. Then a third child wrote down the word *team* while the others helped

him. Everyone on the team was excited to start on the project. I told them, "Tomorrow is another day." And that is how the project started.

Plate 1 shows Ms. Fehr working with the children on their plans for the project. The finished backhoe loader is in Plate 2.

THE NEXT PHASE

Once an idea for the topic has been identified, the young investigators know what they want to know, and the room is prepared with materials and equipment, the class is ready to move into the investigation phase, Phase II.

CHAPTER 3

Developing the Project

With the formulation of a set of initial questions to be answered by the investigation, the project moves into Phase II, which is discussed in this chapter and in Chapter 4. The main features of this phase are the young investigators' in-depth study of the topic, their efforts to seek answers to their questions, and identifying new questions.

BEGINNING PHASE II

As shown in Figure 3.1, Phase II begins with the teacher's reviewing the anticipatory planning webs and the children's web and preparing for the collection of all kinds of data. During the first part of Phase II, preparations are made for the investigative experiences. A field-site is selected. The teacher shares with field-site personnel and expert visitors how children are learning through the project approach and the specific questions the young investigators are asking. Specific investigative skills such as asking questions, using construction tools such as staplers and tape, and observational drawing are introduced to the children along with opportunities to practice them, if necessary.

Reviewing the Children's Web

Many teachers revisit the web or list of initial questions with the children a day or two after its completion. If the web and the list of questions are displayed in the classroom, they may spark additional thoughts as the children go about daily tasks. This happens frequently if the teacher occasionally reminds beginning readers as well as nonreaders of the content of the questions. For example, the teacher might draw a tire next to the question "How many tires are there?" Teachers also make webs more useful for young investigators by attaching photographs or photocopies of drawings to the question (see Figure 3.2). These graphic representations enable nonreaders and younger children to keep the topic in mind in the same way that readers use lists without graphics to recall information. A teacher may add graphic representations of the questions during preparation time, and they are either discovered by the children or presented to the group by the teacher. Children 3 and 4 years old have been observed looking at the list of questions, adding clarification and details to graphics, and even adding more questions. For example, in a project on the school bus, the young investigators were interested in how the door opens when the driver pulls a lever next to his steering wheel. When the teachers sketched the door with the opening mechanism on the question list, one child went up to a drawing, took the marker, and then circled the lever by the steering wheel to show what interested him.

One purpose of revisiting and expanding questions is to encourage children to think in greater depth about the topic. Frequent revisiting of the list of questions throughout Phase II enables young investigators to ask more complex questions as their knowledge grows. However, teachers should not be surprised to find that young children often feel that the questions generated during Phase I are perfectly adequate for the progress of the project. When 3- and 4-year-olds revisit original questions at the beginning of Phase II, often there is no greater clarification or development of complexity of the questions. Revisiting the list of questions with these youngest investigators may still be valuable, however, if the discussion includes new information as the children discover it. Adding to the web helps young investigators understand that their knowledge about the topic is growing. This often brings new enthusiasm to the project topic. However, like everything else, revisiting the original questions can be overdone.

Revisiting the Anticipatory Planning Web

In addition to revisiting the children's web and list of questions at the beginning of Phase II, the teacher can revisit her own teacher instructional planning web,

Figure 3.1 Flowchart of first part of Phase II.

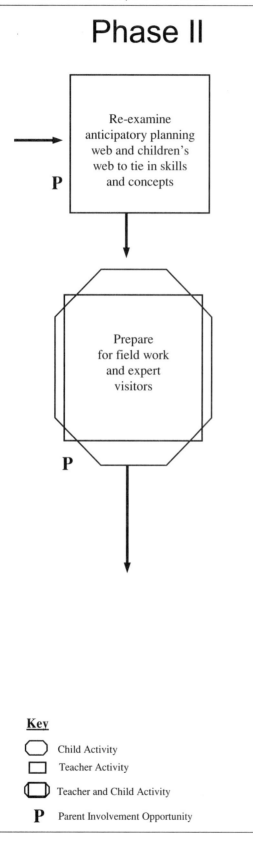

Phase II

Re-examine anticipatory planning web and children's web to tie in skills and concepts

P

Prepare for field work and expert visitors

P

Key

⬭ Child Activity

▢ Teacher Activity

⬭ Teacher and Child Activity

P Parent Involvement Opportunity

Figure 3.2 List with graphic representation for nonreaders.

Nathan
Do all sheep have tags?

Tyra
What do the sheep eat?

Bianca
Where do they live? Do they have a little house or something?

Ryan
Does it hurt to cut the wool?

which was completed in Phase I. Once the teacher is satisfied that there is a good list of questions from the children and that the topic has adequate focus, planning can become more concrete. Some content and questions that the teacher predicted the children might want to know when she made her anticipatory web may now have become the focus of the project. Other concepts on the planning web may have become less important. Sometimes the children focus on a subtopic that the teacher had not anticipated at all. For example, one project began as an investigation of an ice cream store, but children's interests led them into an exploration of milk and where milk comes from. At this point some teachers redo the anticipatory planning web by either circling the main focus on the web and using that as the center of planning or redoing the web if there has been a major unanticipated shift in the project.

As the teacher reviews the instructional planning web, it is also helpful to think about possible representations of the findings of the research. She might try anticipating whether the children might choose to make a play environment, a model, or a mural. In the project on a discount store, the Super Wal-Mart Project, the teacher anticipated that the young investigators might want to create a discount store in their classroom. Because she anticipated this, she was careful to take photos of the aisles, checkout areas, and aisle signs for later reference by the young investigators. As she had anticipated, creating a discount store in their classroom and playing in the store they created became a major part of the project.

Involving Parents

Although some parents may be involved in the project during Phase I, it is at the beginning of Phase II that parent involvement is best solicited. It is a good time to send a letter to parents announcing the project topic and describing the plans with the list of the questions that the young investigators are going to try to answer. A letter can also explain the source of interest in the topic and provide background information regarding the relationship of the topic to curriculum goals for the year. This is another benefit of the teacher anticipatory planning web. The teacher can share some of the content knowledge, skills, and dispositions that she now confidently anticipates will emerge from the project experience. When they begin their first project of the year, many of the teachers whose projects are in this book have shared with parents the handout "How We Are Learning: An Introduction to the Project Approach," which is provided as the last page of the Project Planning Journal at the end of the book.

The beginning of Phase II is also a good time for the teacher to ask parents and others to contribute artifacts and resources for the children to study. Parents frequently will suggest experts or field-sites. Because questions have been clarified and the focus of the project is clear, communication to others at this time in the project can be productive. For example, parents who know that children are asking questions about what a turtle eats, where a turtle sleeps, and if a turtle has toys are unlikely to nominate a visiting expert whose focus might be beyond the young investigators' current understanding. They are more likely to think of the neighbor who has had a box turtle living in his garden for 25 years than of the college professor who studies extinct turtles. Parents can also more easily identify appropriate items or artifacts that would be most beneficial to share with the class. For instance, a parent may have a photo of a pet turtle she had as a child that she can share. Knowing what kinds of information the children are seeking, she might see that her knowledge could make a valuable contribution to the project.

It is also in Phase II that many opportunities arise to extend the learning about the topic at home. Communicating with parents about specific aspects of the project (e.g., the young investigators' questions and current understandings) encourages interactions about the topic between parents and children at home. New concepts about the turtle can become the topic of discussion at the dinner table. Through the discussion parents are then able to reinforce what is being learned and model their own dispositions to be curious and to find answers and solutions to problems.

The effect that knowledge of the project can have on family dynamics when the family is aware of and included in the project is clear in a story from a project about potatoes. Participating in that project was a preschool child who rarely contributed significantly to dinnertime conversations, which were dominated by her older siblings. One evening, however, as the older siblings reported on what they were learning at school, this child launched into a detailed discussion about what her class was learning in the All About Potatoes Project at Bing Nursery School, Stanford University with teachers Jane Farish and Mark Mabry. Much to the amazement of the older siblings and the parents, the child had acquired substantial knowledge of types of potatoes—even beyond that of the adults at the table. The mother reported to the teacher that the dynamics of the family changed forever at that moment, and the young child, instead of being viewed as merely the baby of the family, was now listened to with respect. Many subsequent conversations occurred about potatoes, and the family actually experimented eating different kinds of potatoes.

PREPARING FOR INVESTIGATION

Selecting a Field-Site

Phase II is also the time for the teacher to begin the process of carefully evaluating possible field-sites. Field experiences for projects differ from typical or traditional field trips in certain ways. Traditional field trips are usually taken at the end of a thematic unit, enabling children to see first-hand what they have studied. Traditional field trips also tend to have a broader focus than project fieldwork does. Children may visit the zoo, seeing as much of it as possible in the amount of time available. The agenda for many traditional field trips is planned by the hosts of the facilities visited. For example, a fast-food restaurant might have a standard field trip agenda that they offer to early childhood programs or school groups. The term *field trip* can also refer to simpler, less-focused experiences such as taking a walk around the block. All of these types of excursions outside the classroom can be valuable experiences for young children. However, they differ from the field-site visits that are part of the project approach.

Experiences in the field during project work are specifically designed for the conduct of fieldwork. It is the part of a project that provides children with an opportunity to investigate the field-site, to become engaged in thinking in real depth about the topic. During fieldwork, young investigators attempt to find answers to their own specific questions. They examine closely the field-site and the equipment and materials they find there. They interview people at the site. Young investigators play an active role in capturing the experience through sketching, photographing, or videotaping, so that they may examine and reexamine these records later. They also borrow artifacts to take back to the classroom for further investigation (see Figure 3.3). This kind of field experience requires careful preparation by the teacher. The preparation for the field experience is so important that success of the venture is often determined before the young investigators take the first step out of the classroom. In addition to the teacher's preparation for the experience, children also are included in the planning.

Before the field experience is launched, the teacher helps the children to become clear about which of them will take responsibility for which questions to ask at the site, and who will be responsible for sketching which items, collecting which artifacts, and so forth. One of the teacher's roles during fieldwork is to remind the children of their responsibilities and to support the young investigators' efforts fully.

With very young investigators it is most helpful to select a field-site that will be easy to visit and that will enable multiple visits. That is why field-site possibilities should be considered in the process of selecting the project topic, as explained in Chapter 2. Because young

Figure 3.3 This is a loom that was borrowed by Jolyn Blank's class at University Primary School as part of the Clothing Project. Complex items that encourage discussion and investigation are often loaned to classrooms by visiting experts and field-site personnel.

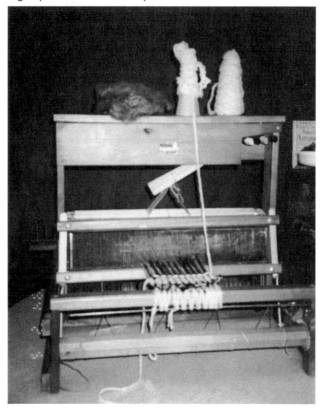

children are often awed by the experience of going as a group to a different location, they may have difficulty focusing on the project topic. Many teachers have had the experience of planning a field trip with young children only to find on return that the most memorable part of the experience for the child was the bus ride. Field-sites that are close enough to the school or center to enable multiple visits have many advantages for projects for young children. If multiple visits are not possible, the teacher will find it helpful to consider seriously how he might capture the field-site to bring it back to the classroom with photographs (both slides and print) and through video- or audiotape recordings. We observed the use of photographic slides for this purpose during visits to the schools of Reggio Emilia.

Some teachers who have successfully used the project approach with young children believe that it is essential to make a preliminary first visit to the field-site without the children. One teacher planned a trip to a radio station without a preliminary visit. When she arrived with her class, she discovered that the studio wasn't large enough for more than a few children at a time, making it extremely difficult for the children to explore, sketch, or spend adequate time looking at the equipment. If a preliminary visit is not possible, the teacher will find it very beneficial to set aside time for an extensive phone conversation with site personnel. An advance visit to the site or extended phone inquiries should provide the teacher with a realistic sense of the potential benefits of the children's visit to the site. In evaluating the site, the teacher should consider the following questions:

SAFETY

- Is the site safe for young children to visit?
- Will it be difficult to monitor the children as they explore the site?
- Will it be possible to shelter children from traffic, machinery, open water, or other dangers?

INVESTIGATION

- Are there areas, processes, or equipment that children can investigate on their own, instead of just hearing someone talk about them?
- Can they climb on, get in, look through, pull, push, lift, press buttons, or make noise at the site?
- Are there any tools, machinery, vehicles, or processes that might capture children's interest and stimulate their curiosity?

CONCRETE OBJECTS

- Does this site have concrete objects with which children can interact? Are there things that can be touched, moved, tasted, smelled, or heard?

- Are there objects that can be sketched or studied closely by a small group of children?

EXPERTS

- Will there be a host or hostess who can serve as expert and answer children's questions?
- Is there someone on the staff who has children or grandchildren of a similar age or who has experience with young children to be that expert?

ARTIFACTS

- Are there any artifacts (tools, equipment, products, and so forth) that can be borrowed and brought back to the classroom for further investigation?

By asking these questions in the preliminary phone call or visit, the teacher begins to form an understanding of the value of this field-site for the children's project.

Preparing Site Personnel

If the teacher has sufficient reason to believe that the field-site visit will be beneficial, she can then proceed with specific plans for the visit. This may occur in follow-up phone calls. A checklist for teachers to use as an outline for these phone calls or visits is provided in the Project Planning Journal found at the end of the book.

It is important to communicate with site personnel about how young children learn. The teacher will want to share the importance of child investigation and discuss how questions will come from the children. Teachers of young children find it helpful to provide an overview of what the children currently know and what they are interested in learning. Site personnel who are not accustomed to having visits of young children may have unrealistic ideas about what questions might be asked. Sometimes it is helpful if the "expert" who will be working with the children on site knows in advance the questions children will be asking, although this is not always necessary. Some experts are more comfortable responding naturally to children's questions. In this case, giving a few questions as examples can inform the site staff of what to expect, yet preserve the spontaneity of the answers to most of the children's questions.

It is also important in this discussion to share the importance of child investigation and the spirit of inquiry. One teacher has found the following phrases helpful:

Our children are learning how to

Ask their own questions
Use experts for resources
Find out answers for themselves

The teacher will also want to share her belief in the importance of children's capturing the site and bringing it back to the classroom to study, especially if a return visit to the site is not possible. It is helpful for the site hosts to know how children will be recording what they learn. It is a good idea to tell the site host if you will be using audio or video recording or photographs and why they might be necessary. Some sites such as banks do not allow videotaping. It is also helpful if the site personnel know in advance that young investigators will be bringing clipboards and writing notes and sketching.

Many teachers report that asking on-site personnel about possible items or equipment that children might sketch is helpful. For example, a manager at a McDonald's restaurant suggested bringing out a French-fry basket and placing it on a table for the young investigators to examine and sketch. Another fast-food restaurant manager took the cover off the soda-dispensing machine so children could see the tubing inside the machine. A manager of a bank anticipated correctly that the young investigators would be very interested in the vacuum tubes for the drive-up teller. He made arrangements to have safety cones to close the lane so children could each experience using the tube and sitting in the lane to do field sketches. Once adults understand the level of the young investigators' knowledge and questions, they often begin to join in the spirit of inquiry and provide experiences for children that teachers are unlikely to think of on their own.

Brainstorming with the site host about artifacts to bring back to the classroom is also helpful. The teacher can ask advice about artifacts (tools, equipment, products) that might be borrowed and taken back to the classroom for further investigation. It is advisable to make a clear distinction between borrowing and giving the artifact to the class. Objects that a field-site host is willing to give to a group of young children are usually small and inexpensive and are not very complex or interesting to them. However, a field-site host will often loan expensive and complex equipment when they know it will be returned. Some artifacts loaned to classrooms for projects include

- A complete set of firefighter's protective clothing
- A bicycle (which the shop owner disassembled in the classroom with the children's help)
- The flashing warning light from the top of a school bus
- A mechanic's scooter used to work under cars
- Animals and their habitats (for example, birds and snakes in cages)
- Publications unique to the topic (for example, school bus magazines) (see Figure 3.4)

Figure 3.4 When magazines, journals, and catalogs designed for adults and related to the topic are made available to young children, they often become the children's favorite reading materials. They are used for research and copying words.

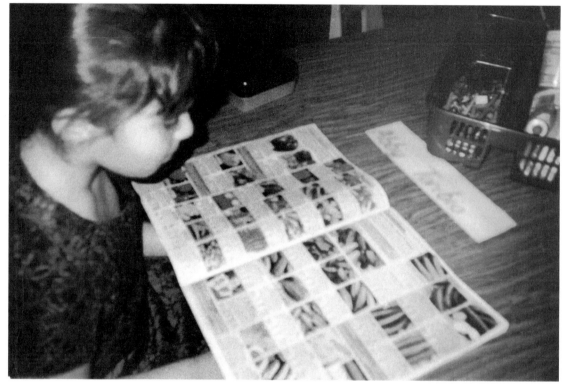

Another reason why it is a good idea to borrow items at the sites rather than receive them as gifts or donations is that many such items could present disposal problem for teachers once the project is over.

Preparing Visiting Experts

Phase II usually includes visits to the classroom by experts on aspects of the topic. These visits to the classroom may precede or follow the field-site visit. Often field-site visits result in additional questions for investigation. An expert can be invited to the class to answer these new questions. The same questioning and brainstorming process that is used to communicate with hosts of field-sites can be used with the visiting experts. Safety issues must also be considered with respect to any items experts might bring with them into the classroom. Such visitors will benefit from the same preliminary information concerning what children already know and what they want to know about a topic. A checklist of items for discussion for visiting experts is also included in the Project Planning Journal.

In Phase II of the projects, support from a librarian becomes even more useful than earlier in the project. Even if the librarian has been contacted in Phase I while children are building background knowledge about the topic, he can be contacted for additional or more specific books again after the questions for investigation have been formed. It is helpful to take the time to share with the librarian the list of questions that the young investigators have generated for investigation and the class webs. In addition to the information that is shared with field-site hosts and expert visitors, librarians also find the instructional planning webs of the teacher informative.

For some teachers, taking the time to share this information with a librarian has resulted in locating books very specific to the focus of the project and even additional resources such as Internet sites and videos. It is important that the librarian also understand the importance of children's being able to actively seek answers to questions and to use books as resources independently. Because young investigators gain much information from studying books with photographs, drawings, and diagrams, books that have these are extremely valuable for projects. Unless teachers share how young investigators can use books as resources, some librarians may not realize that books designed for older children or adults can be just what a 3-, 4-, 5-, or 6-year-old investigating a project will need. A frequent comment from teachers who have used the project approach with young children is how surprised they were to find their young children spending significant amounts of time studying adult materials such as professional magazines that have photos on their topic. During one project, a building contractor's magazine was the most popular book in the book area.

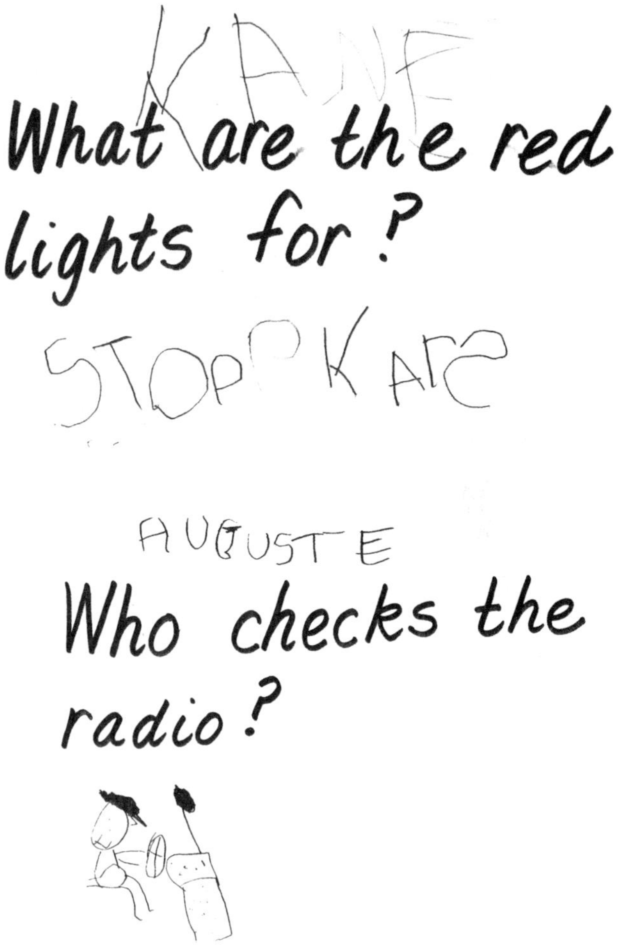

Introducing Skills to Young Investigators

There are many skills that children will use in Phase II of a project. Some of these can be introduced and practiced before they are needed for investigation. One skill that young investigators often need is how to pose a question to an adult, especially an adult who is not well known to them. Most young children in an environment in which they are listened to and encouraged to explore will naturally ask questions. However, young children do not usually know that what they are doing is asking questions. They are often confused when someone asks them "Do you have any questions?" Teaching what a question is can be accomplished informally as children use questions:

Jason: Where is the red dinosaur book?
Teacher: That's a good question. Let's see if we can find an answer for you. Let's ask Matt that question. I saw him looking at it earlier this morning. Matt, Jason has a question for you.

The first time a group of young investigators conducts a field-site visit, some teachers have found it beneficial to practice asking specific questions planned in advance. On field-site visits, teachers usually put questions, or drawings that represent questions, on file cards or papers that are attached to clipboards to remind children what they are to ask (see Figure 3.5). In a simple role-play, the teacher or another child pretends to be the adult, and the child asks his or her question by "reading" it from the clipboard. Through this process children begin to see how speaking loud enough to be heard is important and how they can use their clipboards to remind them of what they wanted to say. It is important not to overdo this rehearsal and not to communicate to young investigators that the only questions that can be asked are those that were thought of in advance and put on their clipboards. Children should also be encouraged to ask questions spontaneously. It is also helpful if teachers remind children of the role-playing experience just before they make the field-site visit. The younger the child, the more beneficial this rehearsal can be.

On field-site visits, young investigators often want to obtain information that deals with quantity. The young investigator is especially interested in how many objects there are of a given kind or in a particular place. Many of the questions that are generated by children

Figure 3.5 These clipboard sheets show how teacher Linda Lundberg wrote the children's questions and how the children recorded their answers on the field-site. One child recorded the answer by writing, the other by drawing. Recording answers benefits from practice.

about a project topic include "how many" questions. For example, in the Fire Truck Project the young investigators wanted to know how many ladders there were on the fire truck. Many young children can learn to use simple tallying or graphing, even at age 3. This can be practiced in the classroom where young investigators indicate tally information about their classmates or their preferences. For example, children may tally the number of tennis shoes in the classroom, or survey the class to determine favorite kinds of ice cream. Four-year-olds frequently begin to write numerals with the tally marks. Simple, quick graphing and charting activities can be added to the classroom on a routine basis so that children are able to practice them and become skillful.

Another skill that young investigators use is observation. Young children are natural observers. However, looking at a particular object for a specific purpose at a specific time may require some preparation. Teachers often provide practice in this skill by taking the class on a walk around the school or center, encouraging the children to talk about what they see as they see it, and then, when they return to the classroom, talking in a group about what they saw. One teacher has found that taking a small group on a walk to the office where the secretary shows them how the photocopying machine works and answers their questions is excellent preparation for field-site visits.

Field sketching and observational drawing are also skills that can be introduced and practiced before a field-site visit. If children make observational drawings of objects on a daily basis in their classroom, then observational drawing and field sketching become productive ways to record observations rather than one of many novel experiences on a field-site.

Observational drawing may be added to the classroom by placing an object and paper, with clipboards or without clipboards, in the art area. Teachers can also model drawing by sitting down and doing their own drawing. The purpose of teacher modeling is not to show children how to draw but to demonstrate the act of looking, drawing, and redrawing. Taking small groups with their clipboards to other locations in the school to make field sketches is also good practice. For example, children can sketch the office or the office equipment. Smith and the Drawing Study Group (1998) provide additional ideas for how observational drawing can be introduced to children.

Another skill that young investigators use in Phase II is taking photographs. Children as young as 3 have taken photographs at a field-site. Each photograph was the responsibility of a specific child. When the children are as young as 3 years old or have coordination problems, adults carry the camera and give it to the child when it is time to take the photograph. Photography is also a skill that can be practiced. It is worth the price of a roll of film to give children a chance to practice taking pictures. A teacher might provide this experience by taking the class around the school and letting each child take an assigned photo. Sometimes teachers put these practice photographs into a book on "our school." Children's dictation can be added as captions to the photos. A discussion can take place about which photos show the objects in the best way, if they are blurred or clear, and if the photographer was close enough to the object. The result of this experience is project photos that are meaningful to the children. Taking photographs also enables the young investigators to keep their focus on the topic during the field experience.

Another useful skill for young investigators is construction and the use of materials such as tape and glue, and tools such as staplers. Although much will be learned about these materials and tools during project construction, prior experience is helpful. Materials and tools enable children to depict their thoughts about the topic and represent their knowledge by constructing play environments, models, and displays. Again, experience before project work will result in easier and more complex representations. Teachers can provide this experience by providing cardboard, tape, and tools in the art area or construction area and encouraging children to create something of interest such as a house or a car. Children can also be encouraged to collect and add scrap materials to the art area for this purpose.

Clay is a wonderful medium for children to use during projects. Children can make sculptures of artifacts and animals, and even buildings and more complex scenes. However, the young investigators' ability to use clay during projects depends on their familiarity with clay. Teachers will want to take time to introduce clay into the classroom. It takes considerable free exploration with clay before children are ready to use it as a representation medium. Teachers of young children who intend to implement projects with children will also benefit from taking a class on how to use clay. Teachers can learn how to select clay and keep it workable, how to wedge it, and some basic construction techniques such as using slip to join pieces, making and using coils, and making pinchpots. There are some excellent books on using clay with young children that will also provide the teacher with the background knowledge needed to help children succeed with clay (Herberholz & Hanson, 1994; Smilansky, Hagan, & Lewis, 1988; Topal, 1983). Children will also benefit from watching others such as a potter or clay artist use clay. All of these experiences will build children's confidence in using clay so that when they want to use it in projects the skill will be there.

MOVING INTO INVESTIGATION

All of these project skills will continue to develop and grow as the project progresses. Teachers should not feel that most or even many of these preproject experiences are required for a project to move on. It is important to keep the pace of the project moving so that young children's interest can be maintained. As soon as a field-site visit can be arranged or an expert visitor can come in, the young investigators can begin their serious investigation.

CHAPTER 4

Investigation

Chapter 3 outlined the beginning of Phase II, during which preparations for conducting the investigation are begun. The main work of the Phase II, however, is the actual process of investigation conducted by the children. At this point in the project, the questions for investigation have been generated in Phase I, and the young investigators have been prepared for many of the project steps they will now take to find the answers. In addition, a field-site has been selected, and special resources have been added to the classroom for investigation. The young investigators are now ready for the most important component of Phase II—that of seeking answers to their questions and exploring the project topic in-depth.

Investigation activities during this time include visiting the field-site, interviewing experts, exploring artifacts first-hand, and using additional resources such as books. As these experiences occur, the young investigators attempt to draw, write, build, and role-play much of what they have learned. As the children find the answers to their questions and use a variety of media to express their knowledge and understandings, interest may decline and it may be time to move to Phase III to culminate the project. However, frequently new questions for investigation are generated during Phase II, and interest is renewed. This sequence of events—investigation, representation, discussion of what was learned—may be repeated several times (see Figure 4.1). In some projects with young children the new questions that are generated move into a different but related concept and subtopics. Additional field-site visits and expert interviews followed by representation may occur several times before the young investigators' interest subsides and the project moves into Phase III.

FIELD-SITE VISITS

Organization of Fieldwork

During site visits with young children, it is essential to have several adults—parents or other volunteers—to help the teaching staff (see Figure 4.2). These accompanying adults will benefit from being fully informed about what is planned and expected, the main purposes of the site visit, and the children's on-site responsibilities. Adults can be assigned to specific groups of children for some of the activities and given information about the questions young investigators in their groups will be asking, drawings that might be made, and experiences that are likely to occur. The children's clipboards, with paper and a note or reminder of any assigned tasks, may be carried by the adult group leaders in tote bags, or placed together in a large container to be transported to the field-sites. Pencils can be tied to the clipboard or placed under the clip of the clipboard to prevent their loss.

One teacher or other adult may have the responsibility for the camera and a list of photos that the young investigators decided to take. Other adults can carry additional cameras, camcorders, or tape recorders to use for documenting the site visit experience. A large shopping bag or box can be used to bring back to the classroom any artifacts borrowed from the site.

With children 3 to 6 years old, the field trip is often taken at the beginning of the project. Most teachers of young investigators think that making the field-site visit early in the development of a project is extremely important for their young children. Mary Ann Gottlieb emphasizes:

> Field trips are a very important part of projects. Children need to get to the site. I have concluded that the field trip is better at the beginning than at the end, especially for young children who have not had many or varied experiences. Going first is better than building expectations and ideas and then getting there and finding out it is not quite what you thought it was. It makes the topic and the investigation authentic right away.

Asking Questions and Preserving Spontaneity

As we suggested in Chapter 3, for young children multiple field-site visits increase the depth of their

Figure 4.1 Flowchart of second part of Phase II.
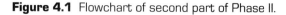

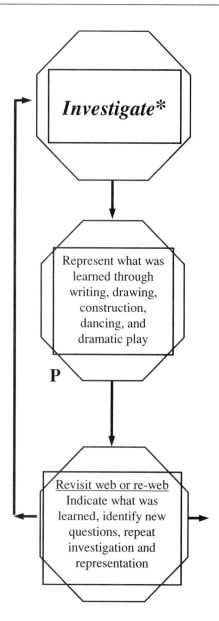

Key

⬡ Child Activity

☐ Teacher Activity

⬭ Teacher and Child Activity

P Parent Involvement Opportunity

Figure 4.2 A parent assisted with the activities of the Farm Project. Here she heads for the bus with the children in her charge.

learning, and more can be accomplished than on a single visit. If there are to be multiple site visits, the teacher plans which experiences to focus on or to provide on the first visit and which to postpone until subsequent visits. Teachers, however, are cautioned to resist the temptation to overprogram the visits. If there is to be only one site visit, teachers have to be especially careful that young investigators will feel free to ask their spontaneous questions as well as those that were prepared in advance and listed on a special piece of paper attached to their clipboards. It is also important that the children be able to take the time to focus on what interests them at the site that might not have been anticipated in the planning before the visit. For example, an early childhood special education class visited a bowling alley as part of a project about balls. While at the bowling alley, several children became fascinated with the ball return and how it worked. They were especially interested in how the ball came up an incline into the rack near them, how it went over a lever that the ball pushed down while passing over it, and then how it was prevented from running back down the incline by the same lever, which had popped back up after the ball had passed. The teacher encouraged them to explore this unanticipated phenomenon as much as they wished.

It is easy to miss these kinds of opportunities for in-depth investigation if the focus of the field experience is only on the predetermined questions and activities. With very young children, it is also important that adults realize that the children may not be able to generate questions about new things that interest them while on the site. For example, asking "Does anyone have any more questions that they would like to ask?" is unlikely to elicit many questions from very young investigators, especially if this is their first project. Teachers and other adults will have to be good observers of children's behavior, watching for signs of interest. Some nonverbal signs of interest are stopping and staring at something, reaching out to an object, and lagging behind the group to spend more time observing or manipulating a particular object. Very young investigators and children who are not very verbal may also indicate interest with the generic question "What's that?" or even simply point to an object.

In the experience with the bowling ball return mechanism described above, when the child pointed to the lever and asked "What's that?" the teacher concluded that this was probably a verbal expression of a number of other questions that the child could not verbalize, such as "What is the name of that? Why does it go up and down when the ball comes over it? What makes it go up and down? Can I push it down? Can I push the ball back over it if I push hard? What if I push it really hard? If I push the ball up the incline and make it roll over it, will it still go down?" When the child was allowed to explore the mechanism physically later, the things that he did with the mechanism inferred he might be thinking these questions. The child's simple statement of interest and his behavior were recognized by the teacher, who then drew the host's attention to it by saying "I think Michael is very interested in this and how it works." Her sensitivity to and interpretation of his behavior to the host enabled greater in-depth exploration.

Sketching on the Site

Ideally the children will have had many opportunities to do observational sketching and drawing in the classroom and around their school or center before they arrive at a field-site with clipboards in hand. Drawing and sketching as part of project work, and especially drawing on site, serve a specific purpose for investigation.

Field sketches involve looking closely at the objects and people studied and making judgments about the parts of

an object, the stages in a process, or the sequence of actions taken by a person. Sketches focus children's attention at the Field-site, which enriches and facilitates later discussion on return to the classroom. (Chard, 1998a, p. 1:11)

Figure 4.3 provides an illustration of this point; a child is carefully studying the wheel of a tractor before beginning to make her field sketch.

Figure 4.3 Observational drawing requires intense concentration and careful study. Focusing on one part of an object, such as the tire on this large tractor, is often simpler for young investigators than trying to draw the whole tractor.

Children often surprise adults with their ability to do observational drawing. Figure 4.4 is a 5-year-old's field sketch of a telephone at the bus barn in Linda Lundberg's School Bus Project. Notice the detail in the drawing of the telephone, the careful attention to shape and size. On the same page, at the same time, the child also drew a person. The person is drawn not from observation but from the child's memory or image of a person. If the drawing of the person is typical of this child's drawing and a teacher were used to seeing this level of drawing from this child, most teachers would not have predicted that this child would be able to draw with such precision and detail. Many teachers report being surprised by children's field sketches and their observational drawings done in the classroom. Observational drawing is also assumed by some teachers to be outside of the range of abilities of 3-year-olds. However, the project work we have observed and that is described in this book provides convincing evidence that this is not the case. Jolyn Blank had guided several highly successful projects with her 6-year-olds. When she began teaching 3- and 4-year-olds, she wondered what she could expect of these young investigators.

Because teachers know what a typical 3- or 4- or 5-year-old can do does not mean that children of

Figure 4.4 When drawing plans for the construction of the dispatch office for the School Bus Project, this kindergartener created a detailed and accurate drawing of the telephone. The person in the same drawing, however, was drawn from memory and is less detailed.

this age should not have opportunities to exceed those limits if they have the desire and have the ability. They might tell you through their work, "See, I'm 4 and even though I might not be able to do this until I'm 5, I just did!" Projects allow for individualization and heterogeneous work. The children can participate on many levels, and on all levels their intellect can be respected.

Figure 4.5 is an example of 3-year-olds' drawings. Some teachers also question whether young children of 3 and 4 are actually representing something symbolically when they draw or sketch as part of their project work. Sylvia Chard has studied drawing in young children extensively and describes drawing as skill that is learned through modeling, being supported, and practicing, similar to how writing is learned.

> There was a time when people thought young children had to learn to write before they could express any of their own ideas in writing; i.e., master the skills of writing before they could use them. Now we know that children can learn to write through writing. The same seems to apply to drawing in our center with the three- and four-

year-olds. Drawing skills and purposeful representation in drawing can develop hand in hand. The double and interdependent satisfactions of improving in both the use of the medium and representation can encourage the child to persist and make rewarding progress in both areas. (Chard, 1998b)

Most of the drawings that young investigators make during field-site visits are observational sketches. However, teachers are often surprised to see that they include details that are not actually there. For example, one child at a farm drew a horse and then put a rider on the horse's back even though there was no rider on the horse he was drawing. The child was drawing not only what he saw but also what he knew about horses from other experiences.

Choosing appropriate objects for field sketching is especially important for the young child just learning to draw. Teachers who have conducted numerous field-site visits with young investigators report that it is more difficult for the children to draw large scenes and large objects than smaller ones. They seem to have difficulty moving overwhelmingly large images onto the small paper. For example, it is easier for them to draw a tractor than a barn when they are just beginners at sketch-

Figure 4.5 Three-year-olds' observational drawings.

ing. For 3-year-olds it is often easier to draw just a small part of a tractor, such as a wheel, than the whole tractor. It is also easier for adults and children to communicate about drawing if the object to be drawn is close to them, and in some cases is one that can be touched and examined in detail.

According to Nancy Smith and the Drawing Study Group (Smith, 1998), it is important not to tell children steps to follow but rather to enable them to construct their own individual drawing strategies. Instead of steps to follow, they suggest a sequence of events to follow in a drawing lesson. This sequence has been helpful to many teachers when they are

assisting children in drawing, especially during a site visit. The following motivational dialogue is suggested.

Ask a question that focuses the children on the topic.
Ask a question that uncovers what they know: *"What is this called? What is it used for?"*
Ask questions to help the child make associations, to clarify ideas and create enthusiasm for the task: *"How are the wheels the same and different? Which part helps you steer?"*
Ask questions that help the child visualize a phenomenon.

Ask a question to help them figure out how to translate responses into marks and lines on paper (not the teacher's solutions; they can be peers' ideas): *"Which parts are connected to the big wheel? How will you draw their shapes?"*

Ask questions that can help children make the transition from looking and help them get started: *"Which part will you draw first? How will you connect this part?"*

In addition to these kinds of questions, Pam Scranton has also found it helpful to draw the child's attention to the paper and get started on drawing by asking "Where will you draw [whatever it is the child has selected to draw]?" "Can you put your pencil where you are going to start drawing a fire truck?" Ms. Scranton's interaction and use of questions to focus attention is included in the documentation of the Fire Truck Project in Chapter 7.

At first when teachers are new to project work with young children, they are reluctant to assist or coach young investigators in drawing during the project. They hesitate to provide guidance especially if in their previous background drawing and painting were viewed as strictly expressive creative media. Using drawing, and later painting, for in-depth study and recording of observations should not be confused with children's free exploration and free artistic expression. Both the representational and the expressive aspects of using graphic media provide valuable experiences and should be encouraged and valued by the teachers of young investigators. Three- and 4-year-olds are more likely to make nonrepresentational drawings and paintings when they are not involved in a project and when their drawing is not intended for a particular purpose, such as observing or recording information. If children understand that all types of expression are valued, they can go back and forth between observational drawing, free exploration, drawing and painting from memory, and so forth, with little difficulty. They appear to take as much pleasure and pride in their experimentation in colors and shapes as they do in their representational work. Drawing and painting are media that children can use to develop a better and deeper sense of their world. They can use them to sort out relationships, experiment with concepts, and communicate what they think. An example of a child using drawing to sort out relationships is 4-year-old Sarah's work on shelves for the Apple Store in Jolyn Blank's classroom. Sarah watches the other children trying to make shelves. She experiments with a piece of cardboard, then finally settles on a construction (see Figures 4.6 and 4.7). Figure 4.8 is Sarah's drawing of her thinking process as she worked out this problem. The first drawing on her page is a top view, and the second is a side view of her final

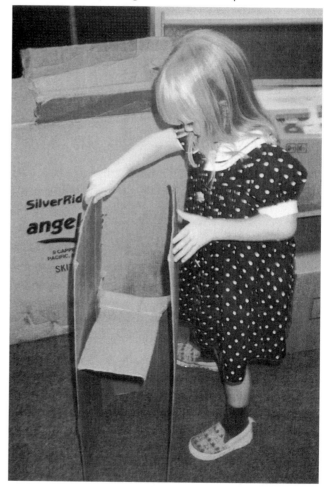

Figure 4.6 Sarah, 4 years old, takes two pieces of cardboard and attempts to get them to stand up to make a shelf.

solution. Drawing helped Sarah think. Around the age of 5, young investigators begin to select themes for drawing or painting and follow through with the theme in a painting or drawing.

Counting and Writing

Young investigators also gather information by counting. Younger children will more than likely use tally marks to gather data, as shown in Figure 4.9. The teacher may simplify the tallying and graphing process by creating a way for children to record data and graph them at the same time. This is especially helpful for young children gathering data on site. A simple way to do this is to make a grid of boxes of equal size. Children can make one mark in the box or color in the box to represent an observation of the objects they are counting, thus using simple one-to-one correspondence to gather and represent quantities. The advantage of using a grid is that the boxes are of equal size, from which

Figure 4.7 This is Sarah's second attempt at making the shelf. She has added more cardboard and a top piece to add rigidity.

children can get a realistic sense of quantitative data by comparing the length of the columns or rows of boxes. If there are older 4s or 5s in the group, these tally sheets can also provide a place for written numerals. The blank tally or graphing sheets are usually prepared in advance and placed on individual children's clipboards.

Young investigators are beginning the journey toward literacy and often have a strong interest in letters on signs and on objects. For example, they often ask, "What does that say?" Field-sites usually provide multiple opportunities to gather printed matter. Most sites have several kinds of signs: Directional, informational, invitational, and warning signs are likely to be readily available. Many objects may have labels on them. Signs can be drawn and letters copied, and children can also photograph signs to be copied in the classroom. If a videographer is documenting the children's experiences, it is helpful to alert him to the importance of capturing the use of letters and words on the site. He can zoom in close enough for children to distinguish letters when they view the videotape on return to their classroom. Adult photographers can also help by observing the same guidelines.

Young investigators also often want to write words right on their observational drawings. If it has been decided in advance that young investigators are going to draw specific items, a word sheet can be placed on the clipboard to enable the children to copy words to label or accompany their field sketches.

Figure 4.8 This is Sarah's drawing and her explanation of her thinking process as she made the shelves.

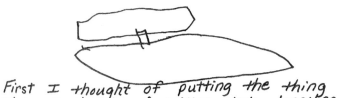

First I thought of putting the thing up.
Then I thought of putting two together.

Then I put them on the thing.

Figure 4.9 This tally chart shows how an adult can take children's questions about a car and provide a way for children to tally the data and also be able to make some meaningful comparison by the number of squares marked.

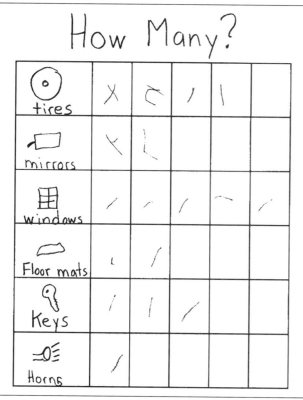

DEBRIEFING

Reviewing Experiences and Field Work

Usually young investigators share what they have learned when they return from a field-site visit. Teachers report that it is helpful to have a general discussion about the trip, so that the children can share what they remembered, what they liked, what surprised them, and what was of real interest. Often this general discussion flows into a rich discussion focused on the investigation. The young investigators talk about what they found out that related to their list of questions or to their web, and to what they wanted to know. Children share the answers they received to their questions, and the teacher adds these answers to the list of questions or to their web.

Young investigators sometimes share other forms of representation during these discussions. These might be tally sheets that they completed during the visits, or sketches they made at the time. Teachers often reserve a bulletin board for these sheets and information to be displayed in the classroom. Often additional questions that emerged from these discussions are added to the

list in a new color, or a new separate list of questions is started.

If photographs were taken, these can be shared as soon as they become available. One teacher of young investigators likes to let the children arrange the photographs on a poster board to show the experience as they perceived it. This creates much discussion and frequently provides a context for the use of new vocabulary. The children sometimes dictate accounts of what is happening in the picture. This kind of discussion not only includes information about what they did during their site visit but frequently includes what they learned. These displays often remain visible for the whole period of time the children are working on the project, and are used to revisit their experiences from time to time. In Phase III, these same sketches and photos may be "published" in a book format to share with parents and others.

Teachers of first-grade or kindergarten children, or even younger children, who are interested in the conventions of writing often take children's dictation about their experience and make an experience chart or a large-size book. By watching the teacher write their words using punctuation and other conventions of print in their story, children begin to develop important understandings about the usefulness of reading and writing. During this process, some teachers also start a "wall of words," such as the one in Figure 4.10, that relates to the project. These words are sometimes written on a large sheet of paper, or some teachers prefer to put these words on file cards that can be removed from the wall

Figure 4.10 This is a project word wall from the Garage Project in Rebecca Wilson's dual-language kindergarten classroom. This word wall was used by children to find out how to write words for their journals, and for other literacy activities related to the project.

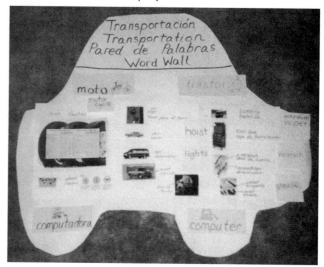

and taken to a table for the young investigators to copy when they want to. Children often nominate new words to be added to the wall.

Artifacts that have been collected during the field-site visit are put out on tables or shelves in the classroom for close inspection. The placement in the room varies by the type of artifact. Some artifacts are placed in the sensory or science area, where they can be touched and manipulated. Empty water tables or sand tables can be used if there is a large number of smaller objects such as car parts. Artifacts that are fragile and will not withstand handling by small children can be placed on pedestals in the art area, and children can be encouraged to observe them without touching and to draw what they see. Some teachers like to keep all project artifacts in one location and create a project table (see Figure 4.11).

Videotapes made during the site visit can be viewed by the children on their return. Some activities that accompany the viewing of videotapes include adding words or comments to their webs and adding words to the word wall. During this period of revisiting the field experience, the teachers also ask children to redraw the items they had sketched on the site. This is most beneficial when it is preceded by viewing of photos, artifacts, or portions of the video that might be relevant. Some young investigators, especially those in kindergarten or first grade, may want to use colored pencils to make

these second or third drawings. Some younger children, however, may be confused by the addition of color at this time and are more comfortable using pencils or fine-line black markers.

This revisiting of artifacts and documentation, followed by drawing and redrawing, occurred a number of times in many of the projects we observed. Some teachers were at first hesitant to ask children to draw the same thing a second or third time. However, they discovered that each time the young investigators revisited and redrew something, they put more and more detail into their representations. Some teachers have found it helpful to have children prepare a drawing; revisit the video, photo, or artifact; and then go back and add more detail to the same drawing. This redrawing may occur the next day or even later. To document the process, a teacher often photocopies the first drawing and subsequent additions to the drawing. She can then capture the growth in understanding and complexity as the child extends her knowledge about the subject and her representational abilities. The successive drawings—whether photocopied or started fresh each time—are commonly called Time 1/Time 2 drawings, and have become especially meaningful to teachers and parents.

Some children may also want to try the medium of paints and use their field sketches as a resource to plan and make their paintings or even to prepare a mural.

Figure 4.11 This is the project table for the garden project at Holy Trinity Lutheran Church Preschool. Most of the items were supplied by a parent when she came to talk to the children and answer questions regarding her garden at home.

One teacher likes to use a photocopy machine to copy young investigators' drawings onto transparencies. These can be projected onto a wall for children to enjoy. The projected images can also be traced onto a large sheet of paper or plastic and children can then paint or color them to make a very colorful and satisfying mural. The documentation (Cadwell, 1997; Edwards et al., 1998; Hendricks, 1997) of these and many other uses of media in the schools of Reggio Emilia has provided inspiration to teachers to introduce children to new materials and new uses of familiar materials. Teachers should not underestimate children's willingness to try new media.

Introduction of Secondary Sources for Additional Research

During this revisiting of the field experience and beginning representation, teachers often introduce additional resources. In many classrooms parents bring in materials for study. For example, parents can contribute new books related to the topic of investigation, documentation that they made during a field experience, or artifacts from sources other than the field-site. These can be shared with the children and added to the classroom materials. If new questions emerge as a result of exposure to these additional resources, they can become the focus of further investigation and plans can be made to find the answers to these new questions. This process might lead to additional site visits or might result in asking specific experts to visit the classroom. Some teachers have been able to take a small group of the children in the class back to a field-site for more in-depth exploration. Parents have also responded to their own children's interest in the topic and taken them to other field-sites. These children then reported back to the class what they learned.

Using New Knowledge in Play

Young investigators often process what they have learned and extend their learning through play. Play can be encouraged by adding props to existing play environments. For example, adding hospital items to a housekeeping area can help transform the play into events related to a visit to a hospital. Play can also be encouraged by making an "instant" environment by projecting 35mm slides of the field-site onto a wall and enabling children to "get into" the experience through pretending. The same effect can be created by making a colored transparency from a photograph and placing it on an overhead projector on the floor and projecting it onto a wall. Young children enjoy changing these images and playing in the various backdrops that they can create with the transparencies.

The creation of play environments by the children became a major focus for young children in projects in this book as they created such things as a fire truck, a store, a restaurant, a hospital room, or a veterinary clinic. When elementary school age children engage in project work, they often create models or displays of what they have observed and learned about. With young investigators, however, the creation of a play environment often becomes the primary focus of the project during this phase. Field sketches, photographs, videos, and books can become resources for accurate representation of the actual place or object for the play-things they create. In the Garden Project at Holy Trinity Lutheran Church Preschool, the children were fascinated by the tiller (see Plate 3) and decided to build one. In Plate 4, the children are studying their photographs. In Plate 5 they are discussing how to add details they noticed in the photographs. Notice the similarity to the real tiller.

Unlike the smaller models that older children make, the young investigators often prefer to create large structures, especially structures large enough for them to get into, and include items that they can use in dramatic play. Plates 6 through 8 show play structures of a variety of vehicles created by young investigators.

Young children who are new to project work or have no previous experience of creating a large play structure are unlikely to think of this option on their own. Teachers are sometimes reluctant to suggest this possibility, preferring to have children develop their own plans. Yet several teachers have supported children's thinking of creating a play environment by providing large scrap materials such as sheets of cardboard or boxes in the classroom and encouraging them to make something with these materials. Other teachers wait until spontaneous play that centers on the project topic emerges; then they encourage the young investigators to create props for the play. They may even suggest materials to use during first project experiences. Once children have experienced a project and have created a play environment, the idea of creating a new structure to use for their play, such as a delivery truck or a restaurant, easily comes to their minds.

Children, just like teachers, learn much about how to proceed in project work by seeing how other children do projects. Project history books and visits to other classrooms where projects are in progress help children build an understanding of the variety of ways they can represent their experiences and findings. Sharing projects within schools or early childhood programs provides not only a forum for the young investigators to report their work, but also a way for other young children to gain vicariously the experience of a project. In this way children acquire some preliminary knowledge of how experiences can be represented. A child may suggest making "a big picture like Mrs. Johnson's class did," referring to a mural he had recently seen in her classroom.

It is in the building of the play environment that much problem solving occurs for young investigators. Older children's project work stimulates them to hypothesize and experiment about relevant concepts. Younger children engage in problem solving as they figure out how to make a window for a bus, or how to make a horse's head stand up straight on their pretend horse, or how to represent accurately what they have observed during their field work. Sallee Beneke (1998) talks about problem solving in Phase II:

> Translating their perceptions into two or three dimensions requires children to consider and select from the media and materials available to them. Depending on her prior experience, a child may have many questions about how to work with these materials, so the product will look the way she envisions it: questions such as, "How do I make it bend? How do I stick it together? How big should this piece be compared to that one? What can I draw on it with? How do I write this word?" Many of these questions stem from problems that arise as the child meets with problems during the course of construction. Social problem-solving is also likely to occur in this phase, if children are working together in a small group to create a representation. They have to agree on what will be done, and they have to reach consensus about who will perform the tasks involved.

An example of social problem solving is given in Chapter 7, which tells the story of the Fire Truck Project in Pam Scranton's class. Two young investigators struggled with making lights for the fire truck that looked both colored and shiny. Two other children who were working on another section of the fire truck critiqued and made suggestions about construction of the lights. Considerable discussion and a willingness to listen to the ideas of another led to the final solution.

Teachers new to project work often have difficulty knowing when they should intervene in this problem-solving process. Sallee Beneke offers this advice:

> As long as children are still trying various means of solving the problem themselves, there is no reason to "step in." I think we are often in too big of a hurry to solve children's problems. If it seems as if they are giving up, then it is probably time to step in. When children are accustomed to using the teacher as a resource, they will often ask for assistance when they really need it.
>
> Sometimes you can tell a young child is getting frustrated and needs help. The child gives up, sulks, walks away, or damages his work (for example, he knocks down his block construction).

Sometimes when I offer help I am pretty direct: "It looks like you're having some trouble getting this to work. Let me show you how to do something that might help you." I try not to give solutions. I try to offer just enough assistance so that the child or children can operate without my assistance again. I try to be honest, respectful, and direct. I try to help the child enough that he can proceed, but not so much that the project becomes mine rather than his. For example, if a child is having trouble connecting two pieces of cardboard with tape, I might say something like, "It looks like the tape isn't holding very well. Other things that we have that might work to hold cardboard are wire, string, or brads. Would you like to try one of those?" If the child asks how to do something, I can demonstrate and/or let him practice on a sample, and then encourage him to apply his new skill on his project work.

Another way that Ms. Beneke supports children's problem solving during construction is by making materials available as she did in the car project. This sequence is documented in *Rearview Mirror* (Beneke, 1998).

> As children began to construct the car, they tried out different types of steering wheels [see Figure 4.12]. Taylor had constructed a steering wheel from sticks and connectors and a circle was cut from tagboard on these attempts. Even with tape the pieces would not stay attached to the dashboard and actually turning the wheel would cause the wheel to fall off the dashboard. It wasn't long before they brought a real steering wheel to the project area. Both children and teachers began to wonder how we could attach the steering wheel to the car so that the children could turn it as they drove. . . .
>
> The student teachers began to discuss among themselves how they might solve the problem. I advised them

Figure 4.12 Taylor tries to make a steering wheel out of tinkertoys.

that if we found a pole or poles that might fit into the steering wheel, we would need to put the pole in with the project materials and give the children the opportunity to discover the solution for themselves.

At home in my basement, I found a pole that I knew would work. I placed the pole in the corner of the project area, and when the children were working on the car that morning I said something like, "You know, maybe one of our car books will show how the steering wheel is connected to the dashboard in a real car." In his typically efficient way, Taylor went to the book collection and found a book that showed the shaft that connects the steering wheel to the wheels [see Figure 4.13]. . . .

Once Taylor decided he needed a pole, he went to the corner and started examining the poles we had collected there. He said, "I think this one will fit," and began to try to separate the duster head from the pole [see Figure 4.14]. . . .

After Taylor had freed the pole, he inserted it into the steering wheel and discovered it was a great fit [see Figure 4.15]. I helped him to cut a hole through the dashboard with a knife. He found that the pole fit through the hole and down into the box next to the motor [see Figure 4.16]. (pp. 28–31)

In this problem-solving sequence, Ms. Beneke supported Taylor by providing resources that he could use to see how others had solved the problem (car diagram in a book) and then by providing materials (poles) within the classroom where children could access them. She was able to scaffold Taylor's problem solving.

Young investigators often solve problems in unique ways. Adults are often surprised at how young investigators sometimes mix a verbal representation into the structure. For example, a silver stripe was represented by sticking plastic knives, forks, and spoons along a line. The children's explanation was that it worked because the items were "silverware." Another young investigator, while constructing a pretend library with a check-

Figure 4.13 Taylor uses books as a resource to find out how the steering wheel works.

Figure 4.14 Taylor takes apart the mop to be able to use the handle for the shaft of his steering wheel.

out system, insisted that books that were brought back should have their cards marked with a red marker because the book had been "read."

Young investigators also often mix play and construction of the play environment. When children in

Figure 4.15 Taylor puts the steering wheel onto the shaft without assistance.

Figure 4.16 Taylor tries out his steering wheel in the car and finds that it works to his satisfaction.

Jodi Knapp's classroom visited the bus barn during the School Bus Project, the children were given the opportunity to see the underside of the school bus by lying down on the mechanic's scooter and being pushed under the bus. When they emerged they did field sketches of the underside of the bus. On return to their classroom, they constructed a bus using a cardboard refrigerator box. One child spontaneously took a long cardboard gift-wrap tube and raised one end of the cardboard box and propped it up with the cardboard tube. He then lay on his back on the floor under the box in the exact position that he had observed the mechanic when under the bus he was repairing, and the same position he had been in while observing the underside of the bus during the site visit (see Figure 4.17).

These play experiences are extremely valuable for young investigators. Through their play, they often consolidate and make deeper and more accurate sense of their experiences and related concepts. As they act out scenarios and roles they observed in their investigations, they make connections between their new knowledge and their own previous experiences and internalize the relevant concepts. Play also creates a purpose for using new words about the project topic so that they become part of the child's active vocabulary.

Projects create opportunities and encourage children to engage in increasingly advanced play. This is especially helpful for children who have not had extensive experience with dramatic play, or who have had a limited range of experiences. Heidemann and Hewitt (1992) present a framework for observing and supporting the development of play skills in children. The framework provides a list of play skills in developmental progression with suggestions for supporting play-skill development. Play skills that are often observed and that teachers can support during project-related play include the following:

- Pretending with objects (real, substitute objects, then imaginary objects)
- Role-playing (using a sequence of play, declaring the role "I am the doctor," imitating actions including dress)
- Verbalizing about the play episode (using words to describe actions, then using words to create a play scenario)
- Persistence in play (staying in a play episode for an extended period of time—10 minutes or longer at age 5)
- Interactions (playing with other children, playing with different partners, playing with three or more children)
- Entrance into a play group (watching what the group is playing, imitating behavior of the group, and joining the play episode)

Figure 4.17 These two photos show, first, the children in Jodi Knapp's preschool observing the mechanic on the scooter at the bus barn; and second, the way the children raised their bus to work on it from the same position.

- Conflict management (using verbal solutions, accepting compromises)
- Supporting peers (offering help, taking suggestions from peers, and encouraging peers)

Many of the higher-level play skills emerge naturally as children become involved in playing roles they have observed during site visits or from the visits of experts who came into their classrooms. Projects can motivate children to become involved in dramatic play and enable teachers to support and coach the development of play skills.

Creating a play structure such as a school bus, or a play environment such as a hospital room, and then playing in it may extend for some time as children make sense of the experience. Representation through play should not be rushed. This is especially true for the younger children, who use play as the primary method of representing their understandings. In many of the projects described in this book, 3-year-olds were often observed representing their understandings and knowledge through play and less often through construction, drawing, or story telling. In the Fire Truck Project described in detail in Chapter 7, 4-year-olds did most of the planning and construction of the fire truck. Although the teacher anticipated extensive rich play by the construction group when the fire truck was finally completed, the 4-year-olds spent only one day playing in the structure they had built. However, 3-year-olds, who had mainly observed the construction of the fire truck, took over the structure and began to play in it, and continued to use the play environment for exploring and revisiting their experiences.

Discussions

Throughout all of these experiences of processing information, the ability of the teacher to respond to children in discussions becomes a critical determinant of how much children gain from the project experience. This is how Barb Gallick, Head Teacher, experienced in guiding projects for young investigators at Illinois State University Child Care Center, thinks about discussions:

When facilitating discussions and participating in discussions with young children, I think I try to continually remind myself not to jump in with an "answer" or give a correct solution to the children. Often teachers hear a child misrepresenting information and feel they need to provide the "right" answer—sometimes they respond without thinking. I try to stop and think for a second before I respond. By doing that, I can make an effort to respond to a child's statement, comment, or question in a way that will extend their thought

and encourage more discussion. I may respond with another question or make a comment suggesting ways we could find an answer to a child's question. Sometimes, I might propose a question to the other children, such as "What do you all think about Joe's idea that a greenhouse is a house painted green?" Hopefully, other children will respond with ideas that might be different—thus encouraging more discussion and sometimes conflicting ideas. If I can draw out conflicting ideas, the group would want to find ways to determine which ideas are accurate, thus setting the stage for further investigations and group work.

My main goal in facilitating discussion would be to draw out the children's thoughts, ideas, and questions so that the children and the teachers could plan experiences that would help us find out more. Early in a project, this goal translates into finding inconsistencies in the children's knowledge of our topic. That's where those conflicting ideas help. We try to ask a lot of "Why do you think . . . ?" or "What do you think about . . . ?" questions. This leads to "How and where can we find out . . . ?" questions.

Later in a project, the goal of drawing out thoughts and ideas becomes more focused on finding out what the children have learned; how their thoughts and ideas have changed; what new questions they might have; and what else they have become interested in about a topic. This type of facilitating is not necessarily new to teachers, but I think in a traditional classroom, it gets lost in the routine of sharing our knowledge with children. I think teachers just beginning to use the project approach really need to look at how they respond to children's statements and questions. They need to focus on improving their technique of asking open-ended questions and making open-ended comments. It is a constant learning experience. I feel I am continually working on my ability to respond in such a way that it extends the children's thinking rather than providing an answer.

Here Ms. Gallick describes an example of a discussion that took place in the center. Lisa Lee and Scott Brouette, additional Head Teachers, are the other adults involved in the discussion.

During the web experience the children made a category of kinds of insects: fly, butterfly, bee, etc., including frog, alligator, and a few other non-insects. We, of course, wrote them down and moved on. Today, the children found a dragonfly in the play yard. We put it in the aquarium. As I carried the aquarium around for all to see, Georgia made an interesting observation.

Georgia (4.8 yr.): The dragonfly and the grasshopper must be related. They both have four wings and probably they both have six legs. Also, my daddy told me that the little things on the front of the spider were part of his mouth.

Breanna (4.3 yr.): They are part of its jaws.

Dylan (5 yr.): They look like snitchers.

Charlie (4.1 yr.): When me and Mikey were climbing the tree we saw this dead cicada shell. We were up in Michigan.

Lucas: We heard cicadas up in the tree at the farm. They were very loud.

Charlie: I saw a Monarch butterfly. I think my white caterpillar turned into it.

Breanna: Really caterpillars don't have wings.

Lucas: Yes, they do. They turn into moths.

Barb: Let's talk some more about what Georgia said about the dragonfly and the grasshopper being related. Can you think of other things that might be related to them?

Emily (3.4 yr.): Spiders.

Breanna: The spider had eight legs.

Barb: How many legs did the praying mantis have?

Kayla: Three on each side.

Lisa: How many does that make all together?

Class: Six.

Scott: Did the praying mantis have wings?

Class: Yes.

Scott: Did the katydid have wings?

Georgia: Yes, it flew.

Scott: How many legs did the katydid have?

Allison (4.11 yr.): Six.

Brandon (3.4 yr.): Ladybugs have wings.

Scott: What about a butterfly?

(We got the dead Monarch off the science table to look at.)

Brelynn (3.11 yr.): It has two wings on each side.

Georgia: That makes four.

(In looking closely at the butterfly the children counted six legs.)

Katie D. (5.3 yr.): I think ladybugs have six legs.

(Brandon got the ladybug model off the science table and Lisa helped him count the legs.)

Brandon: There are six legs.

Lucas: How many legs does a spider have?

(Lucas got some spider models off the science table.)

Lucas: One, two, three, four, five, six, seven, eight.

Lisa: So, do spiders have the same number of legs as the other things we have looked at?

Katie H. (3.10 yr.): No. There are two more legs.

Kayla: Two of them had wings.

Barb: What do we call those things with six legs?

Lucas: Bugs.

Barb: What's that other word?

Georgia: Insects.

After that morning meeting, some children drew the dragonfly while others began to chart out the differences and similarities that had been discussed. We were thrilled that the realization of just what an insect is came from the children themselves. We had hoped to make a chart comparing some of the insects and other animals that had been listed on the original web, but never had the interest of the children when it was offered as an activity choice. Today, though, on their own, they began to categorize and classify, see similarities and differences.

It is important to remember that an alternative choice that these teachers might have made was to simply begin the exploration of insects by telling the children how adults defined insects. This example shows not only how the teachers facilitate the conversation but also how children, even at this age, do not always need to be told information, but—given the appropriate experiences, time to investigate and process information, and an effective teacher facilitator— can develop some very complex concepts on their own.

Project work provides frequent occasions for whole-group and small-group discussions on all aspects of the work. Discussions are contexts in which young children also can sharpen their expressive, listening, arguing, and other communicative skills. Teachers can support and strengthen all aspects of these skills by encouraging children to respond to each other during these discussions. Often teachers of young children inadvertently teach children to speak directly to them, from which the youngsters learn that discussion is just taking turns to have your say to the teacher. For example, one of us observed a teacher of a group of 21 4-year-olds in the early stages of planning a project related to fishing. The children were seated around her in horseshoe formation, and the teacher began, clipboard on her lap, to collect answers to the following question put to each child in turn: "What's your favorite fish?" The first child hesitated a bit and finally offered "goldfish." The teacher responded "That's one of my favorites too" and moved to the next child, who in turn hesitated a while and came up with "I like tuna sometimes," and so on. By the time the teacher reached the tenth child in the semi-circle, the first nine had tuned out, having no investment in what their peers offered. However, the teacher could have encouraged the children to respond to each other, to make suggestions to or ask questions of each other—encouraging cross-child communication.

The capacity of young children to respond to each other is often underestimated. But such communication skills can be learned. For example, the teacher might be informed by a small group that they can't figure out how to represent what they just found out about how many baskets of mail the mail truck delivers each day. The teacher can then encourage a member of that group to raise that question to the whole class and solicit their advice. We have observed children even at the pre-school level willing and able to engage in this kind of joint problem solving and taking considerable satisfaction in being able to help others with their questions.

Taking time to talk one-on-one with children during the project is also important. Scott Brouette shares his thoughts about talking with a child during a project (see Figure 4.18):

Figure 4.18 Scott Brouette shows how listening to children involves patience and attention. He patiently waits for the idea of what to do next with their bug sprayer to come from the child.

Some children are less likely to answer questions or give observations as quickly as others. This is a great opportunity for a one-to-one interaction. In this instance silent thinking is a large part of the interaction. We are both contemplating what to do next with our "Bug Sprayer." With a one-to-one interaction as in this case, it is a lot easier to wait for an answer than with a group of children. Sometimes to help the children that are less verbal it helps to make some suggestions and let them decide from there.

However it is also important for the teacher to realize that there are times not to keep quiet. One of these times is when children need to be encouraged to be accurate, to develop conceptual clarity. Several teachers reported to us a real reluctance to "tell" children anything about the topic. This could result in missing opportunities to open up the topic in a discussion. For example, in a kindergarten project on vehicles, the children revealed that they considered only trucks and vans vehicles. In a situation like this a teacher could ask the children if they would add bikes to the list, and if not, why not. If the children said yes, the teacher could add something like, "Well, what about skate boards or roller blades . . . etc?" and further discussion could be encouraged. The project provides a context for just this kind of dispositional development—the disposition to reflect on one's own assumptions about everyday things, and thereby be motivated to look information up and try to find experts who could clear things up.

MOVING INTO PHASE III

At some point, young investigators begin to run out of questions, and the class and the teacher begin to tire of the topic. Children choose to do project activities less frequently, they look at the project table less, and the project discussions provoke less interest and participation. These are all signs that the project is ready to move into Phase III.

CHAPTER 5

Concluding the Project

There comes a time in the life of the project when children are ready to move on to other things. This can happen for several reasons. Children may simply no longer have questions; their curiosity may be satisfied. Children may also have reached a point at which further investigation requires skills such as reading and writing beyond their current abilities. The topic of the project and the previous experiences of the young investigators can also affect the duration of their enthusiasm for the project. The project may simply have run its course. Sometimes teachers who are new to projects assume that waning interest indicates that the topic was wrong and that the project has failed. They express disappointment as children lose interest and become interested in other topics. However, any topic can be run into the ground! Waning interest is part of the natural progress of a project and indicates that it is time to move into Phase III.

There are three main components in Phase III (see Figure 5.1). For young investigators the main task is to decide what and how to share what has been learned and then to share it. The teacher's role includes debriefing the children and reviewing the project through documentation and assessing the achievement of goals.

CULMINATING THE PROJECT

One of the many benefits of project work comes from the carefully planned, purposeful, and definite culmination of the work. In culminating activities, children begin to see themselves as learners and gain confidence in their ability to undertake investigations and solve problems. Teachers are able to see the results of the project and evaluate its effectiveness with respect to their goals for individual children and the whole group. Good culminating activities also help the parents to see and reinforce the knowledge, skills, and dispositions that were strengthened by the project. The community, if invited to participate in culminating activities, develops a better understanding of how young children learn and greater appreciation for their intellectual abilities.

Focusing on What Was Learned

In the culmination process, the young investigators summarize what has been learned. It is important for children to have the opportunity to "elaborate what they have learned so that its meaning is enhanced and made personal" (Katz & Chard, 1989, p. 84). Articulating what they have learned helps children consolidate and integrate information from different experiences in the project. In Phase III it is just as important to involve the children in decision making as it is in the first two phases. With older children this is fairly easy because they have usually had experience with the options of giving a report, making a book, or preparing a display. With young investigators, these processes and products take time and patience.

The process usually begins with the teacher's asking the children how they might share what they have learned about the topic with others. With young investigators it is helpful to start this discussion by focusing on the web. The teacher may start a new web entitled "What We Now Know." Or the teacher may choose to use the web that children made at the beginning of the project. If during Phase II the teacher added answers to questions and additional concepts to that initial web, he may want to simply review the web with the children and ask for further additions. If the original web has not been changed since Phase I, the teacher may use another color of marker to show what has been learned. It is especially important to record additions to webs or comments during Phase III in a way that they can be distinguished from webs or comments made in Phase I and Phase II so children and adults can easily tell which words and pictures on the web are new.

Talking about what they have learned is easier for young investigators if they can look at their work and other forms of documentation such as photographs and

Figure 5.1 Flowchart of Phase III.

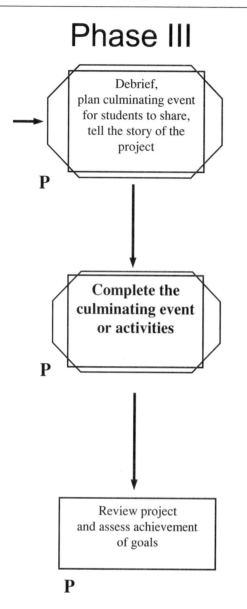

Phase III

Debrief,
plan culminating event
for students to share,
tell the story of the
project

P

**Complete the
culminating event
or activities**

P

Review project
and assess achievement
of goals

P

Key

◯ Child Activity

▭ Teacher Activity

◖▭◗ Teacher and Child Activity

P Parent Involvement
Opportunity

constructions during the discussion. For children from 4 to 6 years old, reviewing the documentation and asking them what they found out and what they now know usually starts a productive discussion. However, children who are new to projects, or children who are not yet very verbal, may be at a loss when asked the question "What did you learn?" They may respond more fully to a question like "What did you find out?" or "What did X tell you when you asked questions about Y?" Starting with a review of the documentation is also a good way for the teachers to support these children. In the process of reviewing documentation the teacher can help children verbalize what they know about the topic. A conversation with a 3-year-old might go like this:

Child: There's Ashley and the ladders.
Teacher: You learned a lot about the ladders. Let's say some things you know about ladders. Fire truck ladders are . . .
Child: Big.
Child: Heavy.
Teacher: Do you remember what the ladders are used for? Fire truck ladders are used to . . .
Child: Climb.
Child: Get people out.
Child: They hang on those hooks.
Teacher: These are things you learned then? Fire truck ladders are big and heavy. Firefighters climb them to get people out. They hang on those hooks.

Another way to elicit what the children have learned is to use some of the same techniques used in Phase I to generate questions. For example, if a book or a large photograph was used as a focus to generate questions in Phase I, this book or photo can be used as a focus for children to discuss what they now know. If there is a wall display of documentation, then conducting a discussion while seated in front of it can also provide a focus for talking about what the investigation uncovered.

Young investigators can be encouraged to represent what they have learned through sketching and drawing. Sylvia Chard (1998a) talks about how drawing can be used in Phase III:

Drawings, especially for the younger children, can be very helpful in enabling them to tell what they have learned. In one kindergarten class the children paired up with their fifth-grade buddies and shared three pictures they had selected from their project folders to explain what they had learned through their project work. The older children were to write what the young children told them about the items in the pictures. (p. 1:13)

Children can be encouraged to prepare a new drawing and put in it everything they have learned about the topic. These pictures can be reviewed and discussed with the teacher and the other children involved in the project. Children can critique each other's work and remind their classmates of details to put in. It is helpful to do this over several days, saving the drawings and adding more details to them each day.

The review and discussion activities are probably the most beneficial parts of the culmination process. As children see more and more words being written on the web, they develop a sense of the learning process. As one kindergartner said, "Wow! We know more now!" As they review their work, they see changes in Time 1 and Time 2 drawings and appreciate their own developing skillfulness. Among the feelings teachers of young children want to engender are feelings of self-esteem and self-confidence. In the course of examining their own growing skillfulness in drawing, for example, children's feelings of esteem and confidence are strengthened in genuine ways. In projects, the children's work, in the form of repeated drawings or attempts to write, is not for "show off." The drawing and writing are purposeful efforts to represent the children's experiences and ideas, in the process of which teachers can encourage them to evaluate their own accomplishments.

At this point, the teacher may want to talk with the children about what they might do to remember this project and what they learned. If they don't have any ideas, the teacher can suggest making a book that tells the story of the project. Sometimes teachers believe that to culminate a project, there has to be a big event. With young investigators, however, activities in the classroom such as making a book about the project, or putting together a bulletin board or a display, may be the most meaningful way to draw the work to a close. The project book may be checked out to parents, who can share it with their children at home. Parents can be invited to view the displays. These provide a sense of closure and enable the children to experience satisfaction from their accomplishments.

If the children have created a role-play environment such as a Pizza Hut restaurant, role-playing in that environment can be a meaningful culminating activity. For example, a group of classrooms at Valeska Hinton Early Childhood Education Center in Peoria studied the local hospital. Each classroom created a part of the hospital in the hallway outside their room (e.g., the x-ray room, the gift shop, and a hospital room). The culmination of this project consisted of providing each group of children with assigned uninterrupted playtimes where they could role-play and enjoy the use of the props in the hospital that they had jointly created.

Sharing with Others

Some projects, however, lend themselves to a more elaborate culmination process. As young investigators become more experienced with projects, they can be encouraged to share what they have learned in a variety of ways. After discussing and documenting what has been learned in the project, the children may be asked what they would like to share with others.

With young investigators, it usually helps to identify a target audience. For example, "What would you like to show your parents about how we learned about the fire truck?" or "Now that you know so much about fire trucks, how about telling Mrs. Brown's class what you did, where you went, and what you found out?" Young investigators who are doing their first project are unlikely to come up with many ideas on their own. The teacher may have to present clear alternatives. Some culminating activities that have worked well with young children include exhibits, pictorial histories of the project, reports, plays, dramas, music, scrapbooks, and school presentations.

In the Fire Truck Project described in Chapter 7, the children decided to make a movie (video) about the process of constructing their fire truck and to invite another classroom to come to a "movie party" and to see the video. This probably came about because this project was documented by video, and the teacher used video to review and extend the field-site visit. The children had become interested in the videotaping process.

In Jolyn Blank's 3- and 4-year-old class at the University Primary School at the University of Illinois, the Tree Project, which included the study of apple trees, culminated in the opening of the Apple Store that the children had created (see Figure 5.2). In projects in which children create a store or a business, the children sometimes chose to actually conduct business on their open-house day. For example, they sell apples or bakery goods or whatever fits with the project topic.

Many projects with young investigators include in the final phase some type of construction that can be shared with others. For example, when a cardboard car was built by the 3- and 4-year-olds at Illinois Valley Early Childhood Education Center, the culminating event was to display the car in the student center (Beneke, 1998). However, projects for young children do not always result in construction. Judy Cagle, teacher of 3- to 5-year-olds at Valeska Hinton Early Childhood Education Center, has guided several projects with young children in which the culminating activity did not include any kind of construction.

The type of culminating activity really depends on the projects—most projects at this age level lend themselves to construction of something as

Figure 5.2 University Primary School apple store.

a culminating activity but some do not. The ones that do not can be just as meaningful and valuable for the children as the ones that result in a construction as long as they have some things for the children to do—to sink their teeth into, so to speak. In my mixed-age classroom we've had a project end in a ballet performance, several end in play performances, and one in museum tours.

Ms. Cagle goes on to describe her favorite culminating event, which occurred when she had a classroom of 4- and 5-year-olds. In a teacher interview, Ms. Cagle described how the children came to create an art museum tour as their culminating event.

The whole project developed from children's interest. We were doing a study (or a unit) on the author/illustrator Eric Carle. We read his books and saw a film on how he makes his pictures. The children got interested in how he made collages. They then wanted to learn to make collages. They made a mural and several children made small individual collages.

At the same time we were reading one of the books about the "box car children" which was about a mystery in a museum. That sparked interest in displaying their work. They started talking about what was in a museum, then they talked about different kinds of museums. The discussion turned to what other kinds of art they could put in the museum. That was the beginning of the art museum project. This lead to an investigation of what a museum is like, what things go into museums, and how objects are displayed in museums.

They ended up with a museum in the hallway. It had their collages, the mural, some watercolors they did of peonies and irises. They made clay sculptures, which we fired in the kiln. One child made a watercolor painting of the *Titanic*, then a clay model of the *Titanic*, and then a Lego model of the *Titanic*. That was all displayed together in the museum. Then they decided to give tours of the museum and that became the culminating event.

Everyone participated in the museum tours in one way or another—making tickets, giving out invitations, or giving tours. They discussed the schedule, how many tour guides were needed for each time slot. Children could sign up if they wanted to be a tour guide, but not everyone wanted to do that. The biggest discussion was on how to rotate the tour guides in the time slots so anyone who wanted to give tours would have a chance to do that. Each child could do as much as he or she wanted. No one was left out because there wasn't a job.

We invited other classes. If a whole class decided to come, the children decided to divide them into two parts. Others who were invited and came were office staff and parents. Several times parents came into the school for some other purpose during that week, and the children would ask them if they wanted a tour and one or two children would give an unscheduled tour.

Ms. Cagle and her aide, Lynn Akers, agreed that the creation of the museum was one of the best culminating events of a project partly because it built on the children's interest in the topic. Ms. Cagle taught the same group of children the following year when some of them had turned 6. She noticed that they used the same planning processes for the culminating event for another project.

They began a project on water. The children created a play about what they knew. It was very meaningful to them, and like the museum, the idea came up first in a discussion and then seemed to naturally evolve into a culminating event. Like the museum, I could see them incorporate all they had learned. I thought it was a great culminating event because the children felt that it was a great culminating event.

Ms. Cagle cautions, however, that culminating activities with an event require careful planning that includes documenting the event.

Plate 1. The children in Natalya Fehr's classroom decided that they needed a work team to construct their back hoe, just like at Caterpillar Tractor Company where many of the children's parents work. Here they are dictating team plans.

Plate 2. This is the yellow team's "backhoe loader," which they made. The process is described in Chapter 2.

Plate 3. This is the tiller that captured the children's interest in the Garden Project at Holy Trinity Lutheran Church Pre-school. They were fascinated by how the tiller would "grind up the ground" to make it ready to plant seeds.

Plate 4. Kara, Rryley, Derek, Megan, and Michael use the photographs of the tiller, such as the one above, as a source for building their own garden tiller, which is located off in the lower right hand corner of the photo.

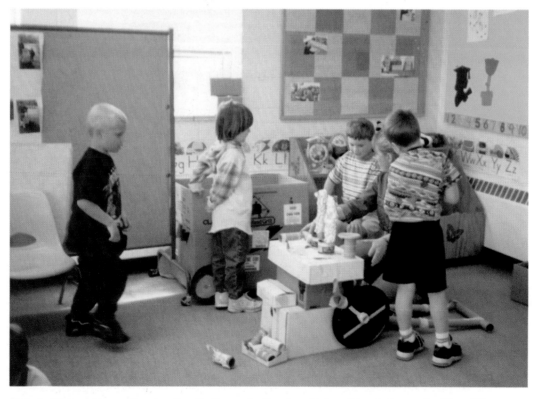

Plate 5. Michael, Megan, Brandon, Pam Podkanowicz (teacher aide), and Derek discuss the tiller, talking about what has to be added and how they might add it.

Plate 6. This constructed bulldozer, like many constructions for projects, becomes a focus for dramatic play.

Plate 7. Children at the Early Childhood Center at Illinois Valley Community College pose for a picture in the car they created during the Car Project. The car is on display in the central gathering place of the college and children serve as tour guides for the construction. Documentation of this project has been captured in *Rearview Mirror* (Beneke, 1998).

Plate 8. Kindergarten children in Linda Lundberg's classroom are finishing up the bus that the morning and afternoon class made during the School Bus Project.

Plate 9. Reviewing photos of field-site visits often helps teachers understand what children are trying to create with their constructions.

Plate 10. This child's cardboard shield and masking tape straps are a representation of the firefighter's equipment.

One problem with culminating events that don't have a product is that they happen and then they are gone and over. We don't have a lot of documentation of the culmination of those projects, like we do the projects where children constructed something. But I know the experience was so meaningful for the children.

Ms. Cagle and Ms. Akers consider these kinds of culminating experiences to be the best culminating events because, as Ms. Cagle said, "I know the experience was so meaningful for the children." Teachers new to projects would be wise to keep meaningfulness to children as one of the major criteria in planning a culminating activity for a project.

Like the events that Judy Cagle describes, many culminating activities involve more than just the children in the classroom and their parents. Culminating activities can be shared with other classes of all grades in the school.

A benefit of culminating events as distinct from other types of culminating activities is that events provide motivation for teachers and children to review skills and consolidate knowledge. Having an event also provides a deadline and a purpose for the culminating work. Preparing and then participating in a culminating event can create enthusiasm in the children and parents. Indeed, one of the major benefits of good project work is the positive way most parents respond to their own children's enthusiasm, involvement, and motivation to work hard. It also provides a sense of teamwork and community as children and parents work together and celebrate together the accomplishments of the project.

Culminating events benefit the young investigators who worked on the project as well as the children who observe the results of their work. Learning to do project work involves complex processes. Children in other classes learn much about project work by looking at other children's projects, especially if they also have a chance to discuss the work with the investigators. They learn how young children can formulate questions for investigation, represent in constructions what they learned about a topic, and plan culminating activities for a project. They see children become more skillful, which increases their confidence that they too will be able to master difficult skills. Early childhood teachers who are learning to use the project approach can form a support network and share project books and documentation of culminating events. This can enable children to see even more of the projects implemented in other classrooms.

Culminating activities can also be shared with the wider community, including those experts and field-site personnel who were involved in the project. Besides culminating events, the community can also be included by having an opportunity to view the documentation of the project. For example, a documentation display on the Drive-up Bank Project from Kay Hughes's first-grade classroom in Harlem School District was put on display for several weeks in the bank, which the children visited and investigated. The Peoria Zoo displayed the Zoo Project documentation panels made by Mary Ann Gottlieb. There are many advantages to broadening the audience of the project, including educating the community about the advantages of active, engaged, meaningful learning experiences such as projects.

THE POWER OF DOCUMENTATION

When a teacher carefully collects, analyzes, interprets, and displays evidence of learning, it is called "documentation." Documentation of projects usually includes observations, collections of children's products, portfolios, self-reflections of the child, and narratives or stories of the learning experience. Documentation may be collected in the form of anecdotal notes, children's work, and audio or video recordings. Children, teachers, parents, and the community can use documentation of projects for a variety of purposes.

There are many reasons that documentation is considered an integral part of the project approach. Comprehensive, good-quality documentation of a project can provide evidence of children's learning in all areas of development: physical, emotional, social, and cognitive. It provides a framework for organizing teachers' observations and recording each child's special interests and developmental progress. Good documentation makes it clear that learning through projects is an interactive process by capturing young investigators' active exploration and interaction with adults, other children, and materials. Documentation also can show how children learn from activities and materials that are concrete, real, and relevant to their lives. Documentation is especially helpful for looking at the kinds of complex integrated learning experiences that are part of good project work.

The most valuable use of documentation in projects with young children, however, may be how it helps guide the teacher in the progress of the project. Documentation that is gathered and analyzed throughout the project enables the teacher to assess what each child knows or can do, and just what materials or activities she is most likely to benefit from next. The teacher can then increase the difficulty, complexity, and challenge of an activity as children are involved with it and as their understanding and skills evolve. Teachers who conscientiously document the children's experiences during projects are more likely to make productive decisions when planning for the project. These decisions include the classroom setup and schedule, what to do next, what questions to ask, what resources to provide, and how to stimulate the development of each child through the project process.

Lev Vygotsky's sociocultural theory explains the importance of teachers' decisions in maximizing learning (Bodrova & Leong, 1996). According to Vygotsky (1978), the teacher is most effective when teaching is directed toward a zone of proximal development for each child. Children learn most easily when the teacher provides experiences within that zone of development. To determine the zone of proximal development, the teacher assesses a child's development in particular skills or knowledge, probes the child's thinking on the topic, and then provides experiences that will build a bridge or a "scaffold" to higher-level thought processes (Berk & Winsler, 1995). Often the most helpful information for the teacher is that which reveals what the child understands only partially, or what the child is beginning to be able to do even if only inconsistently, or what the child is trying to integrate into his existing knowledge. In projects there are many opportunities for young children to reveal their understanding and misunderstanding to the teacher who is observant and vigilant about documenting the children's experiences.

Teachers report that children become aware of the documentation undertaken by their teachers, and it is taken by them to mean that their work is important, worthwhile, respected, and valued. Teachers who carefully document the children's activities have reported that as they increased the attention given to documentation, children became more careful about their work and more evaluative of their own efforts. When teachers document children's first, second, and even third attempts at a task, such as drawing and labeling a bicycle part, children begin to reflect on their own skill development. Children also understand the effect documentation of their work has on adults. Even quite young children are aware, perhaps not consciously, of the positive responses of their teacher and parents to their work.

Documentation of the project in a variety of ways also helps teachers respond to demands for accountability. A strong trend in education is an increase in the demand for accountability, meeting official performance standards, and participating in program evaluation. Schools and other early childhood programs are being required more and more to inform constituencies of the effectiveness of their programs. If the teacher is documenting for program evaluation or to demonstrate accountability, she will want to obtain a copy of the program's goals and objectives or any curriculum guides. Documentation will be most effective for this purpose if it is focused on the knowledge, skills, and dispositions that the school district or early childhood program wants children to develop. Documentation enables the teacher to provide evidence to decision makers and all other stakeholders that learning is occurring as a result of first-hand learning experiences like those afforded by the project approach.

TYPES OF DOCUMENTATION

Most teachers of young children have some familiarity with documenting children's experiences from which inferences can be made about their learning. They may use a developmental checklist, take anecdotal notes, or systematically collect some children's work, such as self-portraits at the beginning and the end of the year. All of these are useful in documenting projects. There are, however, as many different ways to document experience and learning as there are ways that active, engaged children try to make sense of their world. The book *Windows on Learning: Documenting Young Children's Work* (Helm, Beneke, & Steinheimer, 1998a, 1998b) is recommended to help teachers learn how to document.

Teachers who are learning to use the project approach with young children may find it helpful to spend some time studying documentation and the many different ways to document. For example, in a project on the school bus, a teacher might ask a young child to explain a drawing she has made of the bus, but not think to record what the child says in the pretend bus barn. A teacher may record the whole group's questions and comments on the web but fail to record which child said what so that such information could be placed in a child's portfolio. Documenting in a variety of ways enables the teacher to do a better job of getting accurate information about each child. For example, a child who has not developed extensive language skills may be able to draw a picture, or construct a block play environment that shows the depth of understanding the child has about the topic.

Figure 5.3 summarizes the types of documentation discussed in the following sections. Many teachers find it helpful to use this chart to incorporate ways for documenting into their written plans. Thinking in advance about what types of documentation can be collected for different project activities assures that a variety will be used. A fairly common mistake that teachers make in documenting their first project is trying to capture all learning in photographs or to photograph activities for which other documentation has already been gathered. Reviewing the list in Figure 5.3 when planning for documenting can help avoid this pitfall.

Figure 5.3 Collecting documentation in classrooms for young children.

Type of Documentation	How It Is Collected in Classrooms for Young Children
I. Individual Portfolios	Specific content area items collected at specific intervals, for example • Writing samples • Record of problem solving using numbers Unique items that show • Learning style • Interests
II. Products (Individual or Group)	Products that children make or produce such as • Spoken language as collected in anecdotal notes or audio/visual tapes • Written language as collected in signs, captions to photos and drawings, letters, labels, child-made books • Constructions such as play environments, Lego, or block structures • Drawn pictures or paintings • Records of data collection • Musical expressions such as made-up songs or dances
III. Observations	Observations made by the teacher and recorded as • Specific knowledge or skills on a developmental checklist, or curriculum guide • Anecdotal notes on events indicating knowledge, skills, or dispositions • Behavioral indicators of dispositions (expression of interest, time spent on activities, self-selection of activities)
IV. Child Self-reflections	Children's statements of understanding their own • Preferences of activity • Enjoyment or interest in content areas • Pride in accomplishment
V. Narratives of Learning Experiences	Stories of learning experiences of individuals, small groups, or the whole class in • Teacher journals • Displays on projects and units • Books or explanations for parents • Books or stories for children

Adapted from Documentation Web. Helm, Beneke, & Steinheimer (1998a). *Windows on Learning: Documenting Young Children's Work* (p. 36). New York: Teachers College Press.

Observation

Since projects are largely child-directed and teacher-guided, they present wonderful opportunities for observing children. In project work children pose and seek answers to their own questions. They solve problems on their own and with other children and sometimes in consultation with the teacher. As the young investigators are engaged in the learning experience, the teacher is able to watch and observe the children's use of language and their interaction patterns, play levels, and dispositions. These are captured in a variety of ways. The teacher may make anecdotal notes on what he observes noting knowledge, skills, or dispositions. He may use audio or video recordings to document the exact words and actions in a dialogue or problem-solving sequence to analyze later. The teacher may also note what behavioral indicators of dispositions have been observed, such as verbal and nonverbal expressions of interest, choice of activities, and time spent on activities.

These observations can be used as evidence for developmental checklists or for documenting achievement of curriculum goals. Observations and checklists along with children's work products may become a part of children's individual portfolios.

An example of an observation in a project is this description by Sallee Beneke (1998) of 4-year-old Lisa in the Car Project:

> Lisa began at mid-year to attend our center 2 days per week. She had been very quiet and reserved and had taken an onlooker role in classroom activities until we began the Car Project. Most of her participation up to that point had taken the form of vigorous nodding in answer to questions. Lisa volunteered to fill in the "yes" and "no" boxes in the chart to indicate which car parts were actually steel or iron, and which were not. I wrote a model of the two words "yes" and "no" for her and she copied them on the chart in the appropriate places. Completing the chart provided Lisa with a sense of the purpose of print, and she was highly motivated to learn to express herself in writing. Taking on these tasks helped her to find entry into the classroom community. The other children came to appreciate her abilities and her helpfulness. (pp. 36–37)

Projects provide contexts for in-depth learning experiences that extend over a period of time. For this reason they provide opportunities to observe development in a way that captures growth and change.

Collections of Children's Products

Products are one of the most obvious ways to document children's learning in projects. Pictures, webs, musical expressions, constructions, collections of data, samples of emergent writing, and oral language samples all provide effective documentation of the knowledge, skills, and dispositions that develop in project work.

There are many written language products that young investigators produce in projects, even though most young investigators are not yet fluent writers. A 3-year-old may scribble and call it "the doctor's message about the baby being sick." This documents an understanding of how writing is used and the purpose of print. Four-year-olds will often use letter-like shapes for communication. Figure 5.4 shows a child's sign that was a product of a project. The children collected clothing and donated it to a charity as part of the Clothes Project at University Primary School. This is a sign that the children made so that they could sort the clothes into categories to give to the charity.

Young investigators also write letters and other communications in the process of a project. For example, during a field-site visit, the clipboards used by young investigators have sheets of paper on which the questions they are to ask are written. These may be written by an adult with child or adult illustrations. They may

Figure 5.4 The children at University Primary School made signs so they could sort clothes they had collected and give them to a charity.

be written by an adult and then copied by the child. If the child is beginning to sound out words, these may be written entirely by the child. When a child obtains the answer to the question, he will write or draw a representation of the answer. After they return to the classroom, the children read what is on their clipboards as they report back to the group on what they found out about their questions. These answers on clipboards document writing as well as reading. Other written products of projects include books written by children as individuals or by a group of children. Three- and 4-year-olds will dictate words to accompany photos or drawings. Five- and 6-year-olds will often write their own words.

Webs are good products that represent group discussions. When a teacher records children's ideas on a web in the beginning and at the end of projects, contrasting the two webs reveals the growth in the young investigator's vocabulary and the concepts of the topic. Figure 5.5 shows the contrast between what Linda Lundberg's kindergarten class knew about turtles in September and what they knew in October. If the process of making the webs is taped, auditory or visual, or if the names of children are recorded with their comments, the webs can serve as documents of the growth in understanding of individual children as well as the group.

Graphs, charts, tally sheets, and other mathematical representational products also often emerge from projects and can be used as documentation. Figure 5.6 is an example of data collection in a project that documents mathematical thinking. Here children are writing down numbers of items on a school bus.

Figure 5.5 When first webs from a project are displayed next to webs completed after investigation, the growth in concepts is easily understood.

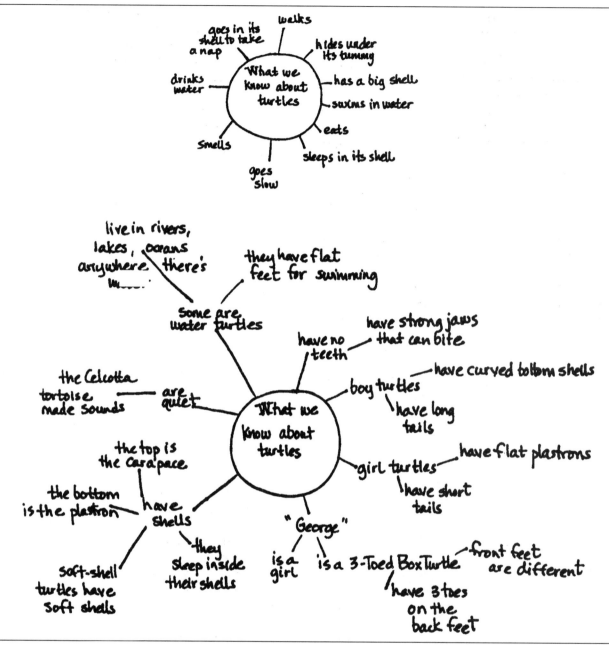

These products can be produced either individually or by a group of children. Occasionally the product speaks for itself, but in general a product's usefulness as documentation can be increased by thoughtful accompaniment of written narrative explaining the significance of the product. In displays of group work, a teacher may choose to select those products that are significant in telling the story of the project or in documenting the development of an individual child through participation in the project. It is not always necessary to display every picture made by every child.

Because the creation of play environments is one of the favorite ways that young investigators explore the project topic, group-constructed play environments are one of the most effective products to use to document children's knowledge and skills. Children build what they know and careful examination of their constructions enables us to "see" what they know. Figure 5.7 shows the bulldozer created by 3- and 4-year-old children at Little Friends Learning Center. One can see in the photo how much the children had learned about the bulldozer just by looking at the construction,

Figure 5.6 Linda Lundberg prepared this sheet for her kindergarten children to record data during the field-site visit.

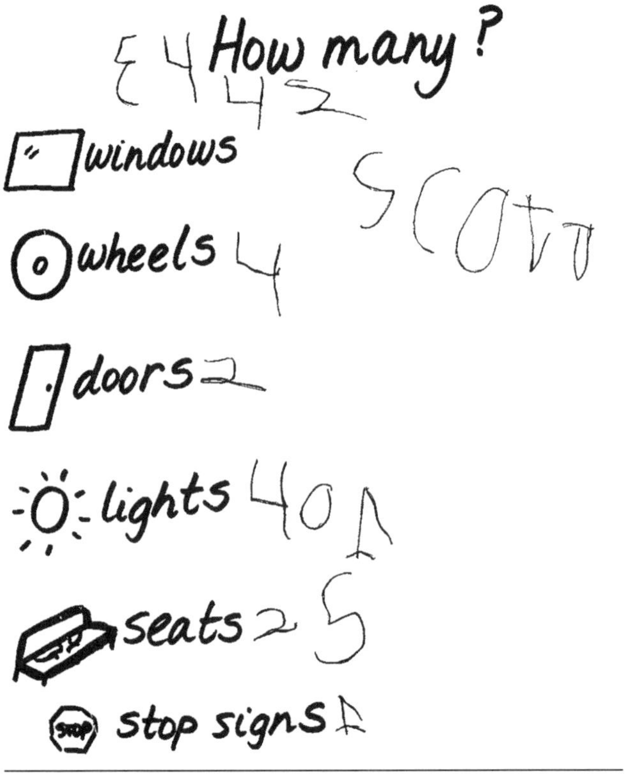

how the children use the construction, and how the construction compares with the real bulldozer in Figure 5.8. It is also possible to see the children's skills in construction and how they solved construction problems.

The extended time and in-depth nature of projects enables rich documentation of children's growth and the development of skills. This is why it is important to make plans to capture children's knowledge and skills at the beginning of a project. This beginning documentation can then be compared with experiences that are documented later in the project. An example of this is the common documentation method of collecting Time 1, Time 2, and so forth, drawings of the same objects observed throughout the period of a project. This documentation is even more beneficial when it is collected from project to project so that it shows children's growth over a longer period of time. For example, Jolyn Blank collected Time 1 and Time 2 drawings by the same children over a period of 2 years in consecutive projects. Figures 5.9–5.13 show the drawings of Edo, a second-language learner as a 3- and 4-year-old. Figure 5.9 shows 3-year-old Edo's first drawing of a tree in the Tree Project. Figure 5.10 is Edo's drawing of a sheep at the sheep paddock. During his 4-year-old year, Edo did these Time 1/Time 2 drawings of the police car (see Figures 5.11 and 5.12). In the first drawing Edo

Figure 5.7 The children of Little Friends Learning Center paid special attention to the detail of the bulldozer that they made.

Figure 5.8 Real bulldozer that served as the model for the children at Little Friends.

could not get all the letters in the space so he wrote only the middle letters of "Champaign." In his second drawing he allowed enough room to get all his letters in. The last drawing by Edo (still 4 years old) is an aerial view of a tricycle (see Figure 5.13). This sample of Edo's work shows how effective this type of documentation can be in understanding children's growth.

Figure 5.9 This is Edo's first drawing at the preschool as a 3-year-old in the fall.

Figure 5.10 The following spring Edo did this drawing of a sheep.

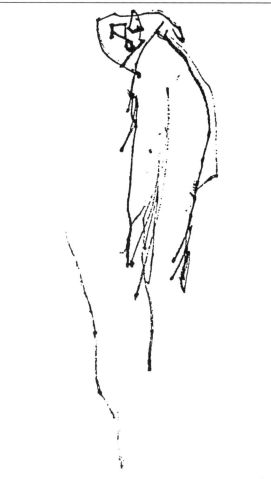

Figure 5.11 As a 4-year-old, Edo became much more detailed in his drawings. On this drawing he attempts to put the letters "Champaign" on his police car.

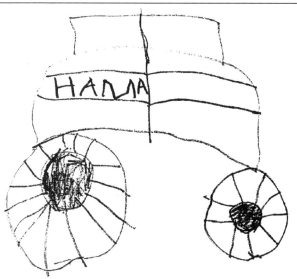

Figure 5.12 In Edo's second drawing of the police car he made the area where the letters would go larger so they would almost all fit.

Project Narratives

Project narratives, or the telling of the story of the project, captures the interest of a variety of audiences. Projects are like a good story. One doesn't always know how a story will unfold or what twists and turns the plot will take. When children are involved in active learn-

Figure 5.13 This drawing in the spring shows how Edo (still 4 years old) is beginning to understand the importance of perspective in drawing. This is a drawing looking down on a tricycle.

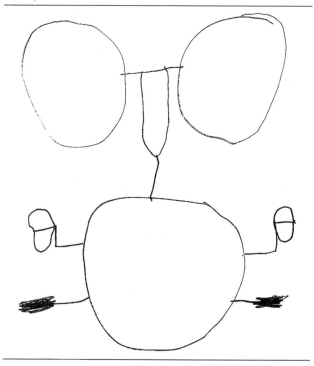

ing experiences like projects, there is an added element of surprise and suspense. Stories are an excellent way to document projects because stories help parents and other adults understand the way that children construct their own concepts and build understanding through their experiences.

When stories are shared as they are evolving, the element of surprise increases the adults' interest in the project and encourages their participation and attention. A tendency of teachers who are new to project work is to gather documentation during a project but to wait until the project is over to analyze and share the documentation. Not only does this make it difficult for teachers to get the maximum benefit from documentation for guiding children's work during the project, but it also reduces the suspenseful impact the project story can have on others.

To capitalize on the evolving nature of the project, teachers sometimes write narratives to accompany wall displays in the classroom or in the hallway outside the classroom. They then continuously update the narrative as children's work proceeds. Photo captions are used frequently to tell the story on these displays. Teachers often share their reflections on the project experience and what they are learning about the children through the project. Children and adults are able to check back with the display to see the progress that the class has made in investigating the topic.

These wall displays are easier to understand if the teacher also displays a project summary. Project summaries assist viewers in understanding more fully what they are seeing. The summary briefly tells the essential story elements of the project similar to a condensed version of a book or a synopsis. It lists the classrooms involved, the names of the teachers, the ages of the children, and the time span of the project. Space is then provided for paragraphs under headings like "Title" or "Focus of the Project," "History of the Project," "What the Children Learned," and "Plans for the Future." A project summary is shown in Figure 5.14 for the Tree Project in Jolyn Blank's classroom. These displays, which share documentation as it occurs, are especially helpful for parents because they enable them to discuss the project with their children. While a project is in process, a summary and handwritten notes accompanying fresh documentation are sufficient to accomplish this goal.

Narratives can also be written for and by children. These narratives are often called "project history books." They usually include photos of the project and the children's words describing what happened. Children's work is also included in project history books. Project history books sometimes focus on only one aspect of a project, such as the building of a structure or the field-site visit. Children enjoy these books, which are made available for them to read and reread and are checked out to parents.

Figure 5.14 Project summary of the Tree Project.

Teachers: Jolyn Blank, Karla Lewis, Betty Liebovich
               University Primary School, University of Illinois
Age Level: 3- and 4-year-olds
Time Span: September-October

Title of Focus of the Project

Trees: We investigated the trees in our playground and around our building. We observed and represented parts of trees, differences among trees and their parts such as shape of leaves, sizes, and changes that occur in the fall.

History of the Project

This project emerged from explorations of found artifacts and field experiences in our immediate surroundings. After creating an initial web of prior knowledge about trees, children began representing the trees around us. Interesting observations of squirrels drawn to a collection of acorns led to further dialogue about trees as homes for animals. Another question for investigation that emerged was, "What comes from trees?" A list was developed that included a variety of fruits that come from trees and children visited an apple orchard.

What did the children learn?

Through the investigation children learned to recognize difference among trees, names of various types of trees, and that it is possible to identify trees by examining the leaves. They identified parts of trees, including the veins in the leaves and the sap and roots of trees. They also thought about the changes that occur in trees in the fall. Some of the children engaged in first experiences with representation and explored a variety of media for representation. In addition, children identified some of the "gifts" of trees, recognizing some of the things that trees provide for people. They learned about a career in forestry and some of the jobs people do at an apple orchard and store. Some of the children looked at the process of growing apple trees, harvesting the apples, and creating products for sale in a store.

Plans for the Future

This project will continue as children complete construction of the apple store. We plan to sell goods from the store. From this experience, we might move into a project about grocery stores.

Project history books are also read in other classes where young children are learning to do project work.

Teachers who do projects with young investigators find it helpful to apply good storytelling principles when sharing narrative documentation about the project. An example of a good storytelling principle is tailoring the narrative to a particular audience. In narratives for parents, the teacher may want to share in-depth information about how the topic fits with curriculum goals. She may want to share her expertise and tell what a particular observation or event indicates about a child's development. In narratives for children, the teacher may choose to focus more on the events of the project and what children saw and did. This enables the children to revisit and reprocess the experience and to see themselves as investigators.

Some teachers have managed to combine these purposes by making displays and books that provide in-depth, content-oriented information for parents at the same time they present the story of the project for children. One way to do this is to put additional information for parents on colored pages or in a smaller type font on the same page. The parent can read the story in the book to the child and read the parent text silently or at another time. Another approach is to put pages for adults on the left-hand side of the book with pages on the right-hand side for children. Parents can read the book to a child easily by focusing on the right-hand pages and come back at another time to study the left-hand pages.

When teachers are doing projects with young investigators, they may find that it is best to provide narratives in the children's own words. This is especially appropriate when children are beginning to understand the function of print or are attempting to figure out the reading process by matching letters with spoken words. It is respectful of the learning process to record in writing the comments or opinion exactly as the child says it instead of editing it for grammar or spelling.

USING MATERIALS AND EQUIPMENT FOR DOCUMENTATION

The teacher planning for collecting documentation should keep in mind the variety of ways to document. A simple planning sheet (see Figure 5.15) can be used

Figure 5.15 Documentation planning sheet.

Anticipated Project Events	Possible Types of Documentation	Equipment or Materials Needed	Collection Task Assigned To	Coverage of Collector's Tasks

to think about the activity of the project, the type of documentation that might be most appropriate for that activity (for example, "observation"), and how it will be documented (for example, "tape recorder in dramatic play area"). Most important, it is helpful to think about who will be responsible for doing the documenting. If the "documenter" normally has a task to do at that time, it is important to think about that task and who can do it so the documenter can be free to proceed with the documentation process. This planning sheet can be ongoing and completed from day to day as the project progresses.

There are many kinds of time-saving materials and equipment that can support documentation in an early childhood center. These include Post-it® notes for writing down observations and folders for collecting children's work and anecdotal notes. Some teachers place pens and notepads around the classroom so that notes can be jotted down quickly right in the area where children are working. Some teachers make sure there is a clipboard for each child, with the child's name on it, and paper. This not only encourages children to write and draw throughout the day but assures that these products can be easily collected by the teacher. A camera with film is essential. A tape recorder can be very helpful, and access to a video camera at certain times during a project can enrich the documentation. Teachers also use a photocopy machine for a variety of purposes. These include to copy children's work that they wish to take home, to reduce or enlarge samples of work so that they can be more easily displayed, and to make multiple copies of children's books or project history books for children to check out and share at home.

When documentation has to look professional, many teachers use a computer with a simple desktop publishing program to make displays and narratives. A scanner greatly simplifies the process of making books, displays, and newsletters. Teachers scan children's work and copy photographs. Children's work can be scanned directly into the computer, reduced so that it is manageable, and shared in a variety of ways. Many teachers find a digital camera easy to use to record project events and to photograph work. Simple digital cameras are now available that can be used by very young children to document the project work. If a multimedia computer system is available, the teacher, older children, or a parent can produce their own multimedia record of projects.

All of this material and equipment is helpful because it encourages documentation and enables the teacher to be more efficient and the documentation to look professional. However, many teachers begin documenting with just a spiral notebook, some note cards, an inexpensive camera, and an organized system for collecting children's work.

DISTILLING DOCUMENTATION

Display panels, transcripts of children's conversations, and project history books have opened teachers' eyes to the value of projects for young children. The polish and complexity of some documentation, however, intimidates some teachers, especially those who are new to the project approach. Much of the documentation that is shared with others is carefully prepared or distilled documentation. Project documentation is collected as the project unfolds and is discussed and shared with others who are working with the children on the project. Only the most informative documentation is "published." Preparing documentation for sharing with a larger audience or for display is referred to as "publishing documentation"—carefully mounting, typing, or displaying. In *Windows on Learning* (Helm et al., 1998b) this process is called "distilling." Sallee Beneke (1998) talks about the distilling process in her center:

In a sense there are really four levels of editing or "distilling" to the documenting we do at our center. The first level takes place as the items are selected for the project board in the classroom. The second level takes place as items are selected and sometimes reformatted for our hallway display. The third level takes place when the documentation is removed from the hallway and panels or history boards are prepared as a final record of our project. This book [referring to the Car Project] in which I have described the project and included samples of the children's work along with my own reflections is perhaps a fourth level. (p. 69)

Detailed advice on publishing documentation and organizing displays is available in *Windows on Learning* (Helm et al., 1998b) and the accompanying *Teacher Materials for Documenting Young Children's Work* (Helm, Beneke, & Steinheimer, 1998a).

Documentation enhances projects with young children, but extensive documentation displays are not necessary for children and teachers to have a successful project or for children to develop new knowledge, skills, and dispositions from the project. The skills of documenting children's work and sharing documentation take time to learn and teachers are advised to set reasonable goals for documenting the first projects they do with young children.

Learning to document can be compared with learning to drive a car: The first attempts are slow, and each step has to be carefully considered and planned. Eventually a driver becomes so skilled and confident that she can drive without consciously thinking about most of the separate tasks, like starting the car. Integrating comprehensive documentation into a project is also a skill that takes time to learn. The teacher who works at improving documentation eventually finds that documentation is so helpful and so natural to the project process that it too becomes automatic.

EVALUATING THE PROJECT

Projects, like all educational experiences, benefit from reflection and evaluation. Guiding projects for young investigators and documenting children's work is sometimes described by teachers as "teaching on the fly." The teacher has to make many decisions during the teaching process in response to children's questions, interactions in the classroom, and children's work in process. The process is a dynamic one. Since *dynamic* is defined by the American Heritage Dictionary as "relating to energy or objects in motion," "characterized by continuous change, activity, or progress," and "marked by intensity and vigor," the term can be accurately applied to the teaching process when the project approach is used with young children.

Teaching on the fly, however, cannot and should not mean that teachers have no goals and objectives, that they have no plan of action, and that they aren't well prepared for the activities of the day. It is important that teachers strive to improve their teaching skills and anticipate where children's interests might be going and how they can best support the investigative and representational processes in which young children engage.

Projects as Engaged Learning

One way to look at the success of a project is to consider whether the experiences it provided were engaging and absorbing, and from which much was learned. Did the learning experience engage children according to the definition of engaged learning described in Chapter 1 (Jones et al., 1994)?

In addition to defining engaged learning, Jones et al. also provided guidelines for looking at various aspects of learning experiences—such as the type of tasks engaged learners do, how learning is assessed, and teacher and student roles—and determining how these would look in a classroom where engaged learning is occurring. The following evaluation questions are based on those guidelines adapted for early childhood programs. Following each question is an explanation of what teachers should look for in analyzing that aspect of project work. The questions are provided in checklist format in the Project Planning Journal at the end of the book.

1. *Do children take responsibility for their own work or activity?* Children demonstrate participation in the processes of the project by asking questions. They "take charge" of the experiences by explaining or showing the teacher what they want to do, and by soliciting the teacher's advice when necessary.

2. *Are children absorbed and engrossed in their work?* Children find satisfaction and pleasure in their work. They appear to be developing a taste for solving problems and deepening their understanding ideas or concepts.

3. *Are children becoming strategic learners?* Children are developing and using problem-solving strategies and skills. They are applying what they learn in one experience to similar experiences.

4. *Are the children becoming increasingly collaborative?* Children work with other children. They talk about their ideas to others. They are fair-minded in dealing with those who disagree with them. Children offer each other support, suggestions, and encouragement. Children are beginning to recognize their strengths and the strengths of others.

5. *Are the tasks in the projects challenging and integrative?* The project is complex and requires sustained

amounts of time and effort over days or even weeks. Tasks require children to stretch their thinking and social skills in order to be successful. Children are learning how components of literacy, math, science, and communication skills are helpful and useful. All children, not just a few, are encouraged to ask hard questions, to define problems, and to take part in conversations.

6. *Is children's work in the project used to assess their learning?* Documentation is collected of how children construct knowledge and create products to represent their learning. The documentation matches the goals of the curriculum. Documentation includes evidence of individual and group efforts. It makes visible children's dispositions such as the disposition to solve problems and to ask questions. Documentation includes drafts as well as final products. Children are involved in the documentation process and encouraged to reflect on the documentation. Children are encouraged to generate criteria such as what makes a good observational drawing or a good question.

7. *Does the teacher facilitate and guide the children's work?* The teacher provides a rich environment, rich experiences, and activities. The teacher encourages sharing knowledge and responsibility. The level of information and support given by the teacher is adjusted based on children's needs. The teacher helps children link new information to prior knowledge and helps children develop strategies to find out what they want to know. The teacher models and coaches. With the children, the teacher becomes a co-learner and co-investigator.

Variations in Engagement

It is doubtful that a teacher will see in one project all the indicators of engaged learning listed above, especially if this is the young investigators' first or even second project. It is also important to realize that all children will not be engaged in all projects all of the time or to the same degree.

One determinant of degree of involvement may be age. Many 3-year-olds are observers of the project process and may float in and out of project activities. These children may experience a project in a way similar to how they experience a teacher-directed unit: enjoying activities, developing some background knowledge about the topic, and sharing some group experiences. They may not at first contribute significantly to generating questions, problem solving, or the kind of in-depth investigation that makes a project different from a unit. However these children are still learning much about the topic through their classmates' work and often become more engaged in subsequent projects. Teachers report that children who participated very little in one project sometimes use skills that they observed other children use but had never themselves practiced, during the next project. Their ability to participate in webbing, to draw, or to ask questions shows that they had followed closely the progress of the project and their classmates' work.

With young children, the degree of engagement is also a function of the project topic. As the teacher is evaluating projects, it is helpful to look at the level at which each child in the classroom has experienced the project. She can then take this factor into consideration of topics for subsequent projects. She can also review the evaluation of previous projects and consider how topic selection can improve the probability that more of the criteria of engaged learning will be met in her classroom.

Besides engagement in learning, there are other factors, such as the achievement of required curriculum goals, that may have to be considered in project evaluation. These may differ from one teacher and from one program to another. Chapter 6 presents a discussion of required curriculum and other issues in implementing the project approach.

Issues in Guiding Projects with Young Children

Once teachers are familiar with the processes of implementing projects and realize how they can support the development of knowledge, skills, and dispositions of young investigators, they then begin to integrate the project work into their curriculum. In this chapter we address some of the main issues related to implementation of the project approach. Depending on the philosophy of the school or center, these issues may be more important for some teachers and programs than for others. Some of these issues concern curriculum requirements, achievement standards, integration of early literacy, involvement of parents in projects, and the use of technology in projects. Other issues involve the use of projects with specific populations such as children with special needs, second-language learners, and toddlers, and the support of administrators for the project approach.

CURRICULUM REQUIREMENTS, STANDARDS, AND PROJECTS

Required Curriculum and Standards

Teachers of young children usually have defined goals for their children and for their programs. These may be articulated in philosophy statements, teaching materials, or curriculum guides. For some teachers of young children, what they offer in their classrooms is determined by local or state curriculum requirement and/or academic standards. In such cases many teachers are concerned about whether they can satisfy the requirements if they use the project approach. It may be helpful before discussing this issue to clarify the difference between curriculum requirements and achievement standards.

Curriculum is defined as an organized framework that delineates the skills and content that children are to learn. It includes the processes through which the curricular goals are to be achieved, what teachers are expected to do to help children reach these goals, and the context in which teaching and learning occurs (Bredekamp & Rosegrant, 1995). The National Education Goals Panel (Goal 3 and 4 Technical Planning Group, 1993) distinguishes between two types of standards: *content standards*, which specify what students should be able to do; and *performance standards*, which gauge to what degree content standards are met—that is, how skilled or competent the student must be.

The project approach is not a curriculum. It does not make up the entirety of learning experiences that the child has in the prekindergarten, kindergarten, or first-grade program. As presented in Chapter 1, there may be many other kinds of learning experiences in classrooms in which projects are also in process. The project approach does not delineate the content that children are to learn. Nor does it prescribe the context for all learning that occurs within the classroom. It provides neither required curriculum content nor content standards.

However, implementing the project approach does not mean that required content and subject matter are excluded from project work. It is quite the opposite: Project work provides a range of contexts in which most significant content and skill requirements can be addressed. Whether the content, subject matter, or topic of a project comes from the children or the teacher, it can usually be related to both content and skills requirements. A characteristic of projects is the emphasis on in-depth investigation, which usually results in children learning a great deal about the topic. It is possible to incorporate many content goals and objectives into project work because of the structure of the approach. The structure of the phases and the emphasis on questions for investigation enable teachers to efficiently plan how they can integrate content goals and assessment into the project experience. This contrasts with less-structured approaches to projects such as project work in the schools of Reggio Emilia, where content goals, performance standards, and early literacy skills are not emphasized.

When required curriculum delineates skills that the child is to learn and practice, the project approach provides many opportunities to apply most academic skills, including speaking, reading, writing, listening, and counting. Some intellectual skills, such as observing, classifying, investigating, hypothesizing, and predicting, are practiced most easily and frequently throughout project work.

Performance standards indicate how skilled or competent children must become. Assessment is usually based on specified performance standards. The specification of performance standards is also compatible with the project approach, especially if evidence of achievement can be gathered in authentic ways, as, for example, through good documentation, which provides rich, accurate evidence of children's knowledge and skills (Katz & Chard, 1996). Project documentation is often a more reliable indicator of what children are capable of doing than are standardized tests, because the high motivation associated with project work results in greater and more purposeful use of their knowledge and skills than tests do.

Using the Project Approach to Meet Standards

When project topics are selected on the basis of the guidelines provided in Chapter 2, the young investigators' learning experiences are often naturally consistent with most content standards and curriculum requirements. Here is a content standard from the National Science Education Standards (National Committee on Science Education Standards and Assessment, 1995):

Content Standards: K–4

Science as Inquiry

Content Standard A:

As a result of activities in grades K–4, all students should develop
• Abilities necessary to do scientific inquiry
• Understanding about scientific inquiry (p. 109)

Content standard A is further clarified in a guide to the content standard:

Fundamental abilities and concepts that underlie this standard include

ABILITIES NECESSARY TO DO SCIENTIFIC INQUIRY

ASK A QUESTION ABOUT OBJECTS, ORGANISMS, AND EVENTS IN THE ENVIRONMENT. This aspect of the standard emphasizes students asking questions that they can answer with scientific knowledge, combined with their own observations. Students should answer their questions by seeking information from reliable sources of scientific information and from their own observations and investigations. . . .

PLAN AND CONDUCT A SIMPLE INVESTIGATION. In the earliest years, investigations are largely based on systematic observations. As students develop, they may design and conduct simple experiments to answer questions. (p. 122)

Teachers who have implemented projects with young investigators report that this content standard is achieved quite naturally in the course of good projects. An example of this is the Turtle Project in Linda Lundberg's kindergarten class at Parker Early Education Center in Machesney Park, Illinois. This project began when a turtle named George was given to the class. The following children's words and drawings about what they were observing are taken from a documentation panel for the Turtle Project.

For several months the children had been caring for George, who turned out to be a girl turtle. In late November she began to act strangely.

What Happened:
The children noticed her digging a lot under her food dish. At times she practically tipped her dish over. We moved her aquarium into the meeting area.

What We Thought and Said:

• She is hungry (P.M. class wasn't feeding her enough).
• Some old food is under the dish and she is trying to get it.

What We Tried:

• We put food in the dish. George didn't eat it. [See Figure 6.1]

When the A.M. class came in, George was partly buried in her wood shavings.

What We Thought and Said:

• George is trying to make a nest.
• George is going to have babies.

Figure 6.1 George the turtle is not eating.

- It is colder. We put on our coats.
- Maybe George is cold.
- He's digging in the chips to get warm.
- She was digging because she was too cold! [See Figure 6.2]

What We Tried:

- We dug our hands into the shavings and into the sand to see if it was warmer (some said yes, some said no).

Figure 6.2 George is digging in the wood chips.

Figure 6.3 Aaron made a house for George. Joe drew a picture of Aaron's house.

- Aaron made a house out of paper for George. George went in. [See Figure 6.3]

What Happened:

   The teacher brought in a log with a hole. George went into the log. George had to be awakened when it was bath time. George wasn't going to the bathroom in her tub anymore.

What We Thought and Said:

- George spends most of her time way inside the log and a little buried.
- George must have been cold and wanted to get warmer.
- The inside of the log was cozy and darker and warmer. [See Figure 6.4]

What We Tried:

- We looked in the book about turtles that we read earlier in the year.
- The children unanimously shouted "George is hibernating!"

This very brief documentation of a small part of the Turtle Project provides evidence that the children in this kindergarten classroom are well on their way to achieving the kindergarten equivalent of Content Standard A, developing the abilities necessary to do scientific inquiry. The documentation shows how children are learning to ask questions about organisms

Figure 6.4 George goes inside his log and hibernates.

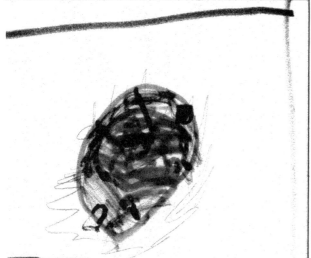

and events in the environment and to plan and conduct a simple investigation. The children's words and drawings could also be collected for documentation of individual children's achievement of the content standard. These could be placed in portfolios. If performance standards were available (i.e., criteria and expectations of what would be considered "good" questions or observations), the children's work could be examined to document those performance standards. Many teachers will find on examining recommended standards in other areas, such as literacy and mathematics, that children are achieving these standards through projects. As teachers become familiar with content standards and required curriculum, they can incorporate the documentation of the achievement of these standards into projects.

Planning for Incorporation of Curriculum and Standards

Not all content standards or required curriculum will naturally emerge from projects and children's interests. However, it is possible to follow children's interests and still be assured that required curriculum is introduced and mastered. Many teachers have learned to follow the lead of children, engage them in learning, and still accomplish curriculum goals. One way to do this is to incorporate required curriculum and standards into the planning process. Many teachers have found the following suggestions helpful:

1. Gather together all statements of curriculum requirements, content standards, and performance standards that apply to the age group being taught.

2. Examine these statements and ask the following questions:

    - What are the knowledge, skills, and dispositions that children are expected to develop?

    - What should the children know and be able to do? If these are not clearly stated, make a separate list and ask for clarification.

    - Are performance standards indicated? For example, if the curriculum goal is for the kindergartener to learn to count, is that rote counting or counting actual objects? How many items should the child be able to count to meet the standard? 10, 20, 100, 1,000?

3. Once the curriculum requirements are understood, watch children for signs of interest that coincide with the curriculum content goals.

    Consider the goals and standards when evaluating the appropriateness of a topic for your project. At the preschool through first-grade level, many of the content goals are stated very broadly. For example, the kindergarten science curriculum may indicate that children should learn about living and nonliving things. What living things do the children find interesting? Are they collecting caterpillars? Are they having many conversations about their pets? These topics have the potential to be projects in which curriculum goals can be easily incorporated. In other words, there is a high probability that children would learn many of the concepts specified in the required curriculum (such as what living things need to survive) in the process of their own self-directed investigation of these topics.

4. Make an anticipatory planning web, first by listing the concepts or content that relates to the project topic.

    The anticipatory planning web in Figure 6.5 shows how a teacher might make a web in response to children's interest in houses. The web shows these concepts in terms a prekindergartener's understanding—for example, that houses are in different styles, sizes, and shapes.

5. Examine the concepts placed on the web in step 4. Add to the anticipatory planning web the required curriculum objectives that could grow from these concepts.

    Curriculum objectives can then be added to the house web (see Figure 6.6).

6. Examine the curriculum objectives added to the web in step 5. Add to the web how the achievement of goals and objectives may be documented.

    A commonly used assessment system at the kindergarten level is the Work Sampling System (Meisels

Figure 6.5 Teacher's anticipatory planning web by concepts (full web shown).

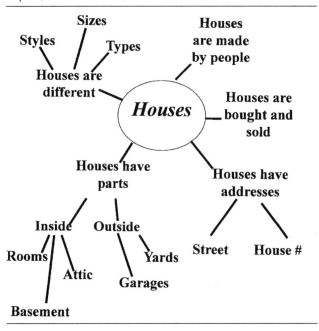

et al., 1994). In the Work Sampling System a checklist is used to record observations of children's development in seven domains of development. Teachers also collect portfolio items. Core items are specific portfolio items that represent particular areas of learning. Teachers in a school determine which items they are going to collect as core items and collect the same type of item three times a year. Core items co-

ordinate with curriculum goals. An example of a core item is a sample of a child's emergent writing. By placing these items on the web, the teacher anticipates where documentation for the portfolio may be gathered to meet performance standards (see Figure 6.7).

Once the anticipatory planning web is completed, the teacher can evaluate whether, on the basis of required curriculum, this topic would be a basis for a worthwhile project. It may not become a project if children's interest wanes. If it becomes a viable topic, then the teacher helps the children form questions for investigation and the process begins.

Thinking carefully about the relationship between the project topic and the required curriculum enables the teacher to introduce appropriate resources as needed and to take advantage of the learning opportunities. It helps the teacher keep content goals in mind as she responds to children during the project process. "Teaching on the fly" as described in Chapter 5 can be more productive.

Seldom, however, does a project develop precisely in the way the teacher had planned in the anticipatory web. The children's interest will gradually narrow, and the main focus may switch to a small section of

Figure 6.6 Teacher's anticipatory planning web showing concepts with curriculum goals added (only part of web shown).

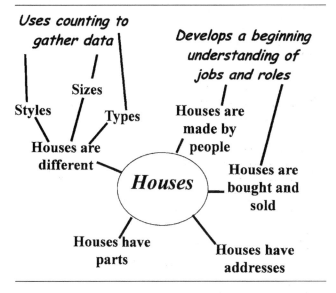

Figure 6.7 Teacher's anticipatory planning web with concepts, curriculum goals, and assessment methods added (only part of web shown).

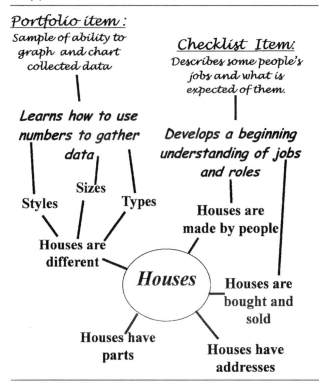

the web, or a new concept not even shown on the anticipatory web. For example, a pet project may turn into an in-depth project about the work of a veterinarian. Teachers at this point may circle the section of the web that is now the focal point of the children's work, and then redraw lines. Sometimes the shift in focus has been so great that a new web is needed. Usually the first web can be cut apart, the new focal point can be placed in the center, and all those pieces of the first web that are still relevant are rearranged around the new topic. At this time the teacher can look at the web and see if there are any concepts or skills that are unlikely to emerge spontaneously from the project work. These can be introduced or taught at other times of the day separately from the project. The teacher may also decide that these concepts and skills might best be taught as a unit or a separate learning experience. Not all content or subjects are best studied through projects.

Integration of Early Literacy Experiences

One area of the curriculum that is more skills- than concept-based is the development of literacy, of reading and writing skills. These skills are learned in many ways, but most children require some formal adult assistance to achieve mastery, and early experiences with books and writing are extremely important (National Association for the Education of Young Children [NAEYC], 1998). Children often learn new skills in reading and writing during the course of a project. Project work also affords many opportunities for reading and writing skills taught in other parts of the curriculum to be applied and therefore practiced. Activities in which children engage during project work are consistent with recommended teaching practices (NAEYC, 1998; Neuman, Copple, & Bredekamp, 2000). Some of these recommended strategies for the preschool years that occur naturally through projects include providing

- Print-rich environments
- First-hand experiences that expand children's vocabulary
- Opportunities and tools for children to see and use written language for a variety of purposes
- Drawing children's attention to specific letters
- Opportunities for children to talk about what is read
- Opportunities to engage in play that incorporates literacy tools

Among the recommended strategies (NAEYC, 1998; Neuman, Copple, & Bredekamp, 2000) for the kindergarten and primary grades that occur naturally through projects are providing:

- An intellectually engaging and challenging curriculum that expands knowledge of the world and vocabulary
- Experiences of being read to and independently reading informational texts
- Daily opportunities and teacher support to write many kinds of texts for different purposes
- Opportunities to work in small groups for focused instruction and collaboration with other children

In addition to recommended teaching strategies, it is helpful to look at developmental milestones in early literacy in relation to the project approach. The National Research Council's Committee on the Prevention of Reading Difficulties (Snow, Burns, & Griffin, 1998) has defined reading and writing skills that should be accomplished during the early years. Some of these accomplishments will require direct instruction for many of the children. However, many of these skills can be integrated into or practiced through project activities. Some that are easily incorporated into project work are listed below.

3- and 4-Year-Old Accomplishments

- Recognizes print in the local environment.
- Understands that different text forms are used for different functions of print (e.g., a list for groceries is different from the list on a menu).
- Uses new vocabulary and grammatical constructions in own speech.
- Understands and follows oral directions.
- Is sensitive to some sequences of events in stories.
- Shows an interest in books and reading.
- Can identify about 10 alphabet letters, especially those from own name.
- Writes (scribbles) message as part of playful activity.
- May begin to attend to beginning or rhyming sounds in salient words. (p. 61)

Kindergarten Accomplishments

- Knows the parts of a book and their functions.
- Recognizes and can name all uppercase and lowercase letters.
- Understands that the sequence of letters in a written word represents the sequence of sounds (phonemes) in a spoken word (alphabetic principle).
- Recognizes some words by sight, including a few very common ones ("the," "I," "my," "you," "is," "are").
- Uses new vocabulary and grammatical constructions in own speech.
- Makes appropriate switches from oral to written language styles.
- Connects information and events in texts to life and life experiences to text.
- Retells, reenacts, or dramatizes stories or parts of stories.
- Listens attentively to books the teacher reads to class.
- Demonstrates familiarity with a number of types or genres of text (e.g., storybooks, expository texts, poems,

newspapers, and everyday print such as signs, notices, labels).

- Correctly answers questions about stories read aloud.
- Independently writes many uppercase and lowercase letters.
- Uses phonemic awareness and letter knowledge to spell independently (invented or creative spelling).
- Writes (unconventionally) to express own meaning.
- Builds a repertoire of some conventionally spelled words. (p. 80)

FIRST-GRADE ACCOMPLISHMENTS

- Uses letter-sound correspondence to sound out unknown words when reading text.
- Reads and comprehends both fiction and nonfiction that is appropriately designed for the grade level.
- Creates own written texts for others to read.
- Discusses prior knowledge of topics in expository texts.
- Uses how, why, and what-if questions to discuss non-fiction texts.
- Describes new information gained from texts in own words.
- Uses invented spelling or phonics-based knowledge to spell independently, when necessary.
- Produces a variety of types of compositions (e.g., stories, descriptions, journal entries) showing appropriate relationships between printed text, illustrations, and other graphics. (p. 81)

Projects are rich with potential literacy experiences leading to accomplishments because reading and writing enhance the investigation process and are used in clearly purposeful ways. Children's motivation to acquire skills seems to be strengthened when they themselves see their purpose and usefulness. As children use books for resources, they begin to recognize letters and words. Books become important sources of information for the young investigator. Literacy artifacts (periodicals, signs, instructions, menus) are also sources of information. Children acquire information from them; they copy words from them and put words on the models they create.

Projects also encourage children to write. They attempt to write because they have a purpose for writing: to communicate across time and from themselves to others. They write questions in order to remember them. They write words on pictures and label parts of things. They write letters to site personnel and experts. They dictate or write captions for photos of the project process. Words on webs are dictated and in kindergarten and first grade are sometimes written by children. They write stories to tell what they learned and to describe field-site experiences. Project topics often appear spontaneously in journal entries. They make "word walls" of words that have importance to them because they tell about something in which they have an intense interest. Writing becomes important to them because they see writing as a tool for their investigation.

Vocabulary develops through children's experiences. The concrete, hands-on nature of learning in project work makes words and concepts more easily memorable. Teachers reported their own surprise at the number and complexity of words that children learn through projects, as in this list of words that the kindergarteners learned in the Turtle Project:

turtle/tortoise
plastron
carapace
bridge
Native American
leg rattles
totem pole
experts
large scale, small scale
shell (soft, hard, top, bottom)
seasonal changes
hibernation
reptile
emporium
three-toed box turtle
mud turtle
stinkpot turtle
African side-neck turtle
soft shell turtle
leaf turtle
ornate box turtle
leopard tortoise
Celcotta tortoise

Teachers, especially kindergarten and first-grade teachers who make projects a part of their curriculum, can maximize the impact of projects on literacy skills. These are some ideas for bringing reading and writing into the project experience.

1. Provide many books and periodicals related to the project for children's use for research.
2. Make "project dictionaries" by cutting photos, drawings, and words related to the project topic from periodicals, catalogs, and brochures. Place them in scrapbooks with labels so children can use them to copy words.
3. Make a project word wall with words related to projects (see Chapter 3).
4. Look for ways young investigators can participate in purposeful writing and reading during the project. At the youngest age level this may be simply putting their names on a survey or placing a check or tally mark on a chart. At the kindergarten and first-grade level, as children develop writing skills, they can write their own lists and write their own questions and answers on their clipboards. They can either

dictate or write letters to site personnel, thank you notes, and letters to other classrooms requesting help gathering supplies or inviting them to a culminating event.

5. Make sure clipboards and words are available for copying. Put a list of project words on children's clipboards for quick reference on field-site visits.

6. Draw children's attention to signs at field-sites. Ask experts to show children how they use writing and reading in their work. Borrow signs, blueprints, brochures, and other literacy artifacts from field-sites.

7. Have children revisit, redraw, and rewrite their work. For example, observational drawings can be photocopied, and the child can use one copy of the drawing for labeling parts.

8. Involve children in the writing of narratives of the project such as project history books, captions for photos and pictures, and wall displays.

9. Suggest possible topics for journal writing that relate to the project topic and especially to individual children's interest in different aspects of the project.

Besides bringing literacy into the project, kindergarten and first-grade teachers can also bring the project topic into other literacy experiences in the classroom. Mary Ann Gottlieb describes some of the ways she integrates the project topic into literacy instruction in her kindergarten classroom at Valeska-Hinton Center:

I always have shared reading that correlates with the project. When we did the Zoo Project, we read the African folk tale of *The Ostrich and Crocodile* [Arademma, 1993] and *There's an Alligator Under My Bed* [Mayer, 1987]. I spend a week on each big book and use it as a reading activity for the week. If I don't have a big book that goes along with a project, then I write one. It may be fiction, folk tale, required reading curriculum—it usually just depends on what the topic is. I don't use a lot of nonfiction for shared reading because it doesn't have controlled vocabulary.

We make lots of little books that relate to the projects. It is a good way to reinforce vocabulary. In the Apple Project, I made an apple tree book that had just the parts of the tree. . . . I used a song as a shared reading activity: five green apples, four green apples, three green apples, etc.

In word lists for projects, I usually make the alphabet and record the words in alphabetical order that go along with the project. It is a graphic organizer; it focuses the children on the beginning letter so it reinforces letter-sound association for children who don't have that yet.

I have two journals for children—a learning journal and a daily journal. In the learning journal we wrote about what we learned about the zoo and about what we saw at the zoo.

We also use the journals for extension activities of the book that goes with the project. For example, we might write about what the children think would happen if there were one more page in the book.

Another way that reading and writing are used purposefully in projects is in the documentation. Children see teachers write their words, they see teachers read their words, and they see the effect of the documentation on their parents and other adults. Children enjoy hearing their words read back to them and seeing the documentation of their project. Reading and writing enable teachers to capture what is happening in the classroom and communicate it to others. This is a valuable use of literacy skills and the importance and the utility of reading and writing are not lost on even the youngest investigators.

INVOLVING PARENTS

In Chapter 1, the advantages of involving parents in projects were presented. There are ample opportunities for parent involvement in projects, and this involvement benefits the parent-child relationship as well as the child's education. A simple group invitation and regular sharing of documentation are enough to build enthusiasm and encourage parent participation in many classrooms. In some programs and schools, however, involving parents doesn't just happen spontaneously in the project process. It takes patience and commitment on the part of the school staff. Some parents may feel uncomfortable in school environments. Going to school and being involved in learning experiences may not be part of the parent's cultural background or may be associated with discomfort in some cultural experiences. There may also be issues of transportation or work schedules. Classrooms in which young investigators are doing projects become communities of learners. Parents can and should be drawn into that community. Teachers are sometimes disappointed, however, when invitations to participate seem to be ignored or parents seem uninterested in the projects or documentation.

Topic selection is especially important if parents are reluctant to participate in the project process. Parents, just like their children, are more likely to respond to project topics that relate closely to their world and what interests them. Adults, like children, appreciate understanding more fully and accurately their experiences and environment. They too enjoy looking closely at phenomena in their environments worthy of appreciation. Parents can become co-learners with their children.

Learning how the suction tube at the drive-up bank works can capture the attention of adults as well as children. Cultural relevance is, however, an important consideration. Parents are more likely to become interested and involved in a project on the auto repair shop down the street than on an ocean that they have never seen.

How the invitation to participate in the project is extended also affects participation. Reluctant parents will sometimes respond to a personal invitation for help rather than a duplicated letter to all parents. When requesting participation, it is also effective to ask parents to help with a specific activity. For example, asking a parent to "come in and show how you make tamales" or "help the children collect acorns in the park" is more likely to get a positive response than asking a parent to just "help out with the project" on Tuesday. A phone call is also usually more effective than a note for many parents.

The teacher also needs to be sensitive to the financial costs of a parent's participation. A parent may hesitate to cook a dish with the children or build a birdhouse if the parent has to supply the materials. When inviting parents to participate, the teacher can also request a list of materials or ingredients that the parent will need and indicate that these will be made available in the classroom for their use.

Sometimes parents who have important knowledge or skills to share on a topic are reluctant to volunteer because they may think their knowledge and skills are inadequate to qualify them as experts. They may not think of themselves as experts or having expertise. Again, parents are more likely to respond positively when the request is clear and specific. For example, a parent may not see himself as someone who can "talk about fixing cars." When a note is sent home asking if anyone can come and show the children how he or she "changes a tire on a car or truck," he may be more willing to participate.

Sharing the questions that children have generated helps parents see the level of expertise needed in the project. Parents are often surprised at how simple the questions are. Knowing questions in advance gives them confidence that they will be able to answer the questions. When parents are asked to "speak to the class" or "share," they often think that means to give a speech. Giving speeches, even in front of small children, is a frightening event to many adults. A more specific invitation that explains what their role will be helps. "Could you come and show the seashells that you and Maria collected at the beach? We'll have you sit at the table and have a few children at a time come and talk to you." As parents get to know the children and feel comfortable in the environment, they often begin to address the whole group.

It is important when parents come into the classroom that the teacher creates an atmosphere of warmth. Many teachers have a procedure for welcoming guests and helpers to their classroom in which the children participate. The teacher or a child shows the adult where to put her coat and where volunteers often work. The volunteer is introduced to the group, and the children are told how to address the volunteer. Children are taught to make a space for the volunteer in whatever group they are in at the time. It is also helpful if the children have laminated name tags that they can slip on whenever a parent or visitor comes to the classroom. Children respond better if the adult can call them by name, and the parent volunteer also can spell children's names if she needs to. These can also be used for field-site visits.

Sometimes teachers have a volunteer basket or tray where they put the materials and tools that the parent might need such as staplers, scissors, tape, and markers. Other teachers have carpenter's aprons with supplies in the pockets that volunteers are given when they come in. Most parents are reluctant to interrupt the teacher if they run out of things to do or need materials. Baskets, boxes, or aprons prepared for the volunteers communicate that their visit was anticipated and valued and that they, like others before them, have a place in the classroom. Giving the reluctant parent something to do immediately also makes the parent feel he is needed and his time is being well spent.

It is helpful to have adult size chairs in which parents can sit and work with the children. Early childhood teachers and young children are floor-sitters, but many parents are not used to sitting on the floor and feel uncomfortable if they are expected to do that. A chair for a 3-year-old is not appropriate for a 200-pound adult male.

When using parents as helpers on field-site visits, following the guidelines in the Project Planning Journal and in Chapter 3 will make the experience not only more productive for children but better for parents. Parents will have a more successful experience and be encouraged to participate again when the teacher takes the time to prepare for their involvement. The teacher can brief parents using the checklist in the Project Planning Journal and carefully select children assigned to each adult. The teacher should keep the more challenging children in her group. Documentation of the experiences at field-sites in photos and display panels should include not only what the children do, but also what parents do. In this way other parents can see how parents were involved and what they did.

For a variety of reasons, some parents are not able to assist with a project during the school day. These parents can be asked to contribute specific items for the project. We have worked with several teachers who have engaged young children in projects of shoes. In each case parents have seemed more than willing to donate old shoes, boots, and slippers to the children's collection for study. They can undertake a particular activity at home and send documentation to school. For example, the report of an examination of the pipes coming into their kitchen or bathroom can be sent to the class. Documentation such as project history books can be sent home. If the program is multilingual, it is helpful to have all languages spoken by the group of children included in the project history book.

Care should also be taken to schedule culminating events at the most convenient times. Having a culminating event in which children must be present and where parents are encouraged to bring extended family members often brings parents to school. Once there, they can view documentation and talk with other parents about the project.

It is especially difficult to get parents involved in projects if this is the first project for a class or even a school. Once parents become involved in a first project, they understand the process and often become more responsive and involved in subsequent projects. Pam Scranton contrasts the Fire Truck Project, the first project for that classroom, with the Vet Project, done by the same young investigators later in the year.

> Our parents had really bought into the project approach. There were so many donations from parents for the vet clinic. They had experienced projects, they knew what they were about, what the children were trying to do. They brought things in. Our parents brought in stethoscopes, white nurses' coats which the children labeled vet coats, empty bottles that the children covered and labeled "cow vitamins," old brushes and combs for the grooming center, empty shampoo bottles. One mother brought in an old hose sprayer from the sink. That was a main part of the washing spot that the children made. One mother supplied us with all the boxes we needed. The children brought in stuffed animals for the patients. When we did the Fire Truck Project I had to request everything, but on the Vet Project the parents understood what it was about and spontaneously brought these things in. I never made a list. The children made a list of what they wanted and told the parents. It was wonderful to see that happen. The children were dying to build this vet office. The children became the catalysts for the parents.

The teacher who is having difficulty getting the participation of parents in a project can take heart from Pam's story. Documentation, patience, and the building of a

history of projects can bring parents into the learning community.

UTILIZATION OF TECHNOLOGY

Many of the teachers whose projects are described in this book have become highly competent at utilizing technology in the project process. New technology skills used by these teachers have ranged from less sophisticated skills such as how to use the photocopy machine to more elaborate skills such as how to make multimedia presentations on the children's project work. In many cases, the projects provided an impetus for the teachers to make great leaps forward in their technological skills. Teachers often reported working with and learning from parents. Together they used technology to improve the quality of the learning experiences in their classrooms.

Photocopy machines were used by teachers of young investigators in instruction and documentation, as mentioned in Chapter 5. Photocopies of artifacts and photos, black-and-white and color, were used to make project dictionaries, to illustrate words on webs, and in narratives and displays. Children's drawings were copied mid-process so that the sequences of the drawing process could be captured. Teachers copied children's drawings so children could label them without writing on their original work. Multiple copies of project narratives and children's conversations were made for portfolios. Several teachers reduced children's drawings and sketches so that much of children's work could be included on one page or in a book.

Teachers also used the photocopy machine to better utilize the overhead projector, which became a permanent piece of equipment in many of the early childhood classrooms where projects were being done. Some teachers made color transparencies of photos to be projected on walls so that field-sites could be revisited and experienced again. Colored transparencies made of children's work were projected and discussed by large groups of children. These were also used as backdrops at culminating events. At the Illinois Valley Early Childhood Education Center, black-and-white transparencies were made to project children's sketches on large paper so the children could trace them for murals. The young investigators were able to manipulate their drawings on the overhead to place them on the mural where they wanted them to be. Children also were encouraged to draw directly on transparencies with markers for projection.

Many teachers, who took more and more photographs for documentation and to use for revisiting experiences, became interested in what makes a good photograph. They studied photography and learned how to use the zoom feature of the camera and how to select different speeds of film, and some learned to use a digital camera and to upload the images to their computer.

Tape recorders and video cameras became commonplace in many of the classrooms in which young investigators were working. Pam Scranton used tape recorders and video recorders for documentation and to "capture" the field-site and bring it back to the classroom for study in the Fire Truck Project. Young investigators in several of the classrooms learned to operate the tape recorders and VCR themselves. They would often play a videotape of the field-site visit when they wanted to check something. Several of the teachers invested in small handheld tape recorders, which they could place near children, or in remote microphones so they could more accurately capture conversations.

Computers were used for many purposes by children and teachers in the Car Project at Illinois Valley Early Childhood Education Center. They were used as tools for children and teachers to record their thoughts. Four- and 5-year-olds were often involved in typing words for signs or letters into the computer. In Rebecca Wilson's bilingual kindergarten classroom, the children designed their own computer form for the Kindergarten Garage as part of the Garage Project. The form was used to record information from the customer when they brought the car to the garage to be fixed.

Many of the teachers mastered desktop publishing programs and incorporated scanned work of children into newsletters and project books. Ruth Harkema created memory books for the School Bus Project by scanning and copying photos so that each child could have one to keep and take home. Some teachers learned how to make PowerPoint presentations for project documentation, and some even put project histories with children's work on school websites.

Because young investigators learn best from hands-on experiences, computer programs and the Internet were used less for their research than they were used by older children who are adept at reading and writing. However, teachers and parents often found articles in multimedia CD-ROM encyclopedias or on Internet sites, which they then showed to children. Many teachers used the Internet and encyclopedias for sources of photographs and diagrams. Sites with full-screen photos were popular as were web cams, Internet sites where a video camera continuously projects the same scene. A birdfeeder cam enabled children to watch birds come to a birdfeeder in a different state.

Teachers are beginning to use technology to help young investigators communicate with experts and with other young investigators. Four teachers from two school districts in central Illinois conducted projects with their children on the same topic. Mary Ann Gottlieb and Judy Cagle taught 4- and 5-year-olds in Valeska

Hinton Early Childhood Education Center, an urban school. Stacy Berg and Pam Scranton taught for a special education association in Washburn and Eureka, rural communities. All four of these classrooms studied the farm, each class going its own direction. The young investigators shared questions, drawings, and information through the Internet. At a culminating activity at Valeska Hinton the children met, shared their work, and participated together in activities related to their Farm Project. Pam Scranton says this about the project:

> The young investigators benefitted by expanding their own growing knowledge about the farm by listening and responding to their peers. . . . Eureka children were given the chance to hear about dairy farming and to study the dairy farm model, Valeska-Hinton children observed and sketched the tractor constructions, and Washburn children observed the outcome of the chicken incubating. During project work, it's important for young children to learn to listen to each other, to make constructive comments, and to join in group discussions. The children got many chances to practice these skills during the culminating activity [see Figure 6.8]. Also, some of the more rural families were given the opportunity to experience an urban school in a very positive light.

USING THE PROJECT APPROACH WITH SPECIFIC POPULATIONS

The authors are often asked if the project approach is appropriate for all children. Questions usually focus on the appropriateness for young children who are 3

Figure 6.8 Children work together and share their common interest in the farm.

and 4 years old, or children with special needs, or children who come from backgrounds that have provided only limited educational experiences. Sometimes teachers indicate that they believe the project approach is appropriate for children from advantaged homes but not for children who are growing up in poverty and who need practice on skills. The implication is that not all children are capable of doing in-depth investigation or that projects take time away from other badly needed direct-instruction experiences. One teacher examining drawings and observations of 4-year-olds in a project commented that these children were obviously gifted and that is why they were able to do the work they did! However, this was not the case. The children were actually in an early childhood program designed for children at risk of academic failure.

As discussed in Chapter 1, the project approach may be especially meaningful for children growing up in poverty and many of the projects in this book come from intervention programs for young children at risk of school failure, many of whom are also poor. Although this book focuses on the effectiveness of the project approach for 3- to 6-year-olds, in the following sections we will address the appropriateness of using projects with particular groups of children: those with special needs, second-language learners, and toddlers.

Children with Special Needs

Many teachers think that projects are not appropriate for children with special needs, or children with "special rights," as they are described in the schools of Reggio Emilia (Edwards et al., 1998). However, we have observed many projects done in classrooms where children had special needs, both self-contained classrooms and others with full inclusion. Rebecca Edmiaston (1998), who has studied the use of projects in inclusive environments, concluded that the project approach is particularly well suited to meet the needs of all young children. She lists five reasons for this claim. The first is that projects are collaborative; that is, they encourage children and teachers to work collaboratively and all children to contribute in their way. Second, projects are based on children's interests. She tells this story of a project in an inclusive environment.

In a class meeting children in an inclusive kindergarten were exploring "shoes" as a possible next project. To the casual observer a young child with disabilities was squirming around on the floor looking at his feet and apparently was not engaged in the group discussion. His behavior probably would have been described as "off-task." However, his teacher recognized that he was tracing the lines on the soles of his shoes as the other children were identifying questions they had about shoes. She pointed out to the children that he was examining the pattern on the bottom of his shoes. His activity captured the interest of the others and they quickly began to examine their own shoes and those of their peers. As a result, several children became very interested in how patterns and different colors and words were imprinted on tennis shoes. Children made representations of the bottoms of their shoes and some even tried to make their own shoes. The child with special needs was able to address one of his educational goals, identifying similarities and differences, through his interest in the different patterns he found on the bottoms of shoes. (p. 1:20)

In project work, children's interests are encouraged and the learning experience can be shaped to meet all children's needs. Third, in projects not all children do the same things. Projects include a variety of experiences and activities. They do not require that every child participate in every experience so individual abilities are taken into consideration and individual educational plans (IEPs) can be integrated. Fourth, much work in projects is undertaken in small groups, which makes it easier to be sure that individual goals are met and that the child with special needs can be included. Fifth, the rich documentation and the emphasis on documenting the children's activities and experiences in the variety of ways that children learn and express themselves facilitate the emphasis on their strengths. Throughout this book, we have shared ways that teachers determine interests through observation, encourage verbalization from children who are not yet verbal, and support children to use a multitude of ways to investigate. These are all good techniques for use with children with special needs.

Second-language Learners

Projects can be most helpful for another group of children: those who are learning a second language. In U.S. schools, this primarily includes children who are learning English and native-English-speaking children who are learning second languages in bilingual or foreign language immersion programs. Many experiences that occur in the typical process of a project are compatible with recommendations for second-language learners. Teachers can use the project approach to help them meet language goals for these children. Pérez and Torres-Guzmán (1995) emphasize the importance of authentic literacy events in the early years—reading and writing that is meaningful and purposeful. They also recommend beginning with children's interest and planning around a "theme": "Students' interests are the best place to begin curriculum planning" (p. 70). Others stress the importance of cultural sensitivity in second-language instruction (McLaughlin, 1995; NAEYC, 1995). Focusing projects on the children's immediate environment and the interests of the children and their families helps achieve this goal. Pérez and Torres-Guzmán's recommendations also include purposeful collaborative learning and culminating activities, which occur as a natural part of the project process.

Many of these recommendations are rooted in the importance of hands-on concrete experiences for learning. Christian (1994) says that for bilingual classrooms "experiential or hands on learning works especially well because students can get meaning from experience as well as from language"(p. 10). Christian also suggests that graphic representation techniques such as webbing, small-group discussions, and direct experience on field trips help children pick up relationships that might be missed because of language differences. These experiences also reinforce new vocabulary and concepts. Rebecca Wilson teaches a dual-language Spanish/English kindergarten and has just begun to use projects in her classroom. She identifies some of the advantages she has found in including projects in her curriculum:

> Projects help with literacy development in both languages. Children use books and resources in both languages, and they work hard to understand what they say because they want to learn about the topic. When we make up questions for experts they have to think in the language of the expert so they can communicate.
>
> There are many places a child can fit into the project. Children at all different stages of development in their language can find something to do and contribute.
>
> Being a non-native Spanish speaker, I've found that the project also pushes me to use more complex words and sentences in Spanish because the children want to know exact names for things. This helps my Spanish speakers continue their development in their language, which is important, and enriches my English speakers' experiences. For example, in the Garden Project I learned and used names for many different kinds of garden tools—words that I had not learned before—for example, three-tined cultivator. I have come to rely on my parents as resources for this knowledge. In the Garage Project, I had to ask a father to tell me the Spanish words to describe the mechanic's car lift which the children were creating in their garage. My need for parents to help in this way has also made them a part of the process. Parents are interested in the projects and in what we are doing.

Wong Fillmore (1985) recommends strategies for children who are just learning to speak English. Many of these are already part of the project approach or are easily incorporated. Some of Wong Fillmore's strategies are included in the recommended strategies for projects and second-language learners, which follow:

1. *Use demonstrations.* These can occur during field-site visits and classroom visits by experts. Bringing artifacts (such as tools) into the classroom for children to use or incorporate into dramatic play increases the understanding of what was demonstrated.

2. *Model and role-play.* Role-playing how to ask questions of visitors, as suggested in Chapter 3, provides valuable language practice. Creating dramatic play environments encourages role-play and the use of language related to the topic (see Chapter 4), especially if children are involved in creating the environment or play structure.

3. *Provide new information in the context of known information.* Discussing what is known about a topic and using graphic organizers such as webs, lists, and word walls enable children to connect new words and concepts with what they know and what they are experiencing. These are especially helpful for children with limited English proficiency. It is most effective if there is a clear distinction between the two languages in the graphic organizers such as the word wall shown in Figure 4.10, which has English words related to the garage on one side and Spanish on the other.

4. *Repeat words, sentence patterns, and routines.* The extended time frame of projects and the in-depth nature of the investigation support repetition. There is time for children to repeatedly use words, phrases, and sentences in a meaningful way until they become part of the children's language. Incorporating songs, storybooks, and rhymes that relate to the topic also provides repetition of words.

5. *Tailor questions for different levels of language competence and participation.* In the project, children's questions can be as simple as yes/no questions or as complex as "How do they . . .". Teachers can encourage all children to participate in thinking of questions, asking, and recording answers.

Taking care to include these strategies as part of the project activities can help the teacher achieve language goals for second-language learners. It also enhances the benefits of the project when the teacher uses the project experiences as a focus for any individual or small-group support she provides for second-language learners.

Projects and Toddlers

Often when a school or center becomes involved in the project approach, the teachers who care for the toddlers in that program will ask if the project approach can be used with their toddlers. Our first reaction is to answer that 3 is probably the youngest that the project approach might realistically be implemented. This was based on the observation that young 3-year-olds often need a great deal of support in the earliest phases of the project approach. Toddlers cannot engage in creating a web, nor can they usually formulate questions for experts. Also, in multi-age groupings they often tend to float in and out of projects and follow the lead of older 3s and 4s.

However, we have seen toddlers actively involved in investigation. We have viewed documentation showing toddlers' growth in thinking and understanding and heard teacher reports of the enthusiasm with which parents receive reports of the toddler "projects." The activities occurring in these toddler classrooms are not the project approach as defined by Katz and Chard (2000) and described in the flowchart and the examples in this book, but these activities are certainly an in-depth investigation of a topic worth learning more about for the toddlers. Children are actively involved in learning and children are investigating. These toddler projects have these characteristics in common with the project approach:

1. Toddlers are watched for signs of their interests. They show interest nonverbally and verbally.
2. Teachers who see interest in objects or activities (such as balls or shoes) respond by bringing in resources and arranging for field-site experiences.
3. Toddlers learn words and concepts such as *ball* and apply those words and concepts in new situations.
4. Toddlers develop ways of investigating such as dropping, or pushing, or trying to put something through a hole, which they then apply to other objects or items and observe results. They build a repertoire of learning strategies. Teachers challenge toddlers by introducing new resources.
5. Toddlers can recognize themselves in documentation and can recall and discuss experiences.
6. Toddler teachers and parents have found documentation to be a wonderful tool to communicate about the toddler's growth and to provide insight into the growth in quality of thinking.

In addition, toddlers were observed to meaningfully explore, with careful supervision, the affordances of different media such as paper and pencil, paint, and clay. The toddlers respond to the attention given by the caregivers to their interest and their initiative as they explore new items and objects in that environment. Teachers and parents also appear to see the toddlers as individuals with great strengths.

Projects with toddlers appear to look more like the flowchart in Figure 6.9. Significant time is spent in Phase I with a focusing event. Investigation in Phase II appears to be accomplished by providing additional experiences and introducing items into the environment. Activities during this phase sometimes include making project books with photos of items for children to look at and carry around, artifacts introduced into the environment for children to explore, photos and documentation covered with plastic and placed on walls and floors, simple field-site visits where additional experiences with artifacts occur, and some simple experiments where toddlers can do things and observe the effect. For example, the toddlers in Figure 6.10 are exploring how balls go in and come out of pipes. Investigation in projects with toddlers is almost always done as an individual activity or with very small groups of children. Culmination of projects with toddlers is more a teacher activity of summarizing what has happened and telling the story. It also signals a possible change in focus of the teacher in the selection of activities and experiences to provide for the children. This is more appropriate for the toddlers' sense of time and sequence.

At this time, we have not done enough observation and study of these projects to be able to offer advice to teachers who want to try projects with toddlers. Toddler teachers are advised to consult the work of the teachers in infant/toddler centers in Italy (Edwards, Gandini, & Forman, 1998; Gandini & Edwards, 2000; LeeKeenan & Edwards, 1992). However, many of the thoughts that teachers of 3- to 6-year-olds have shared about projects in this book may also be applied to doing "projects" with toddlers.

ADMINISTRATORS' SUPPORT OF THE PROJECT APPROACH

Learning to use the project approach with young children is a complex process. Teachers face many challenges unique to projects at this age level that teachers of older children implementing the approach do not have to address. Many administrators are recognizing the advantages of the project approach for the children in their school or center and are beginning to encourage teachers to attempt to learn the process. Cathy Wiggers has directed an early childhood program in which the project approach was initiated and is currently professional development coordinator at a center where projects have been a part of the curriculum for some time. She supports project work because she thinks it brings about good-quality learning in which children become engaged in the work and aspire to do things well. She likes the way children have the opportunity to become decision makers and take responsibility for their accomplishments. She also sees that in

Figure 6.9 Flowchart of projects with toddlers.

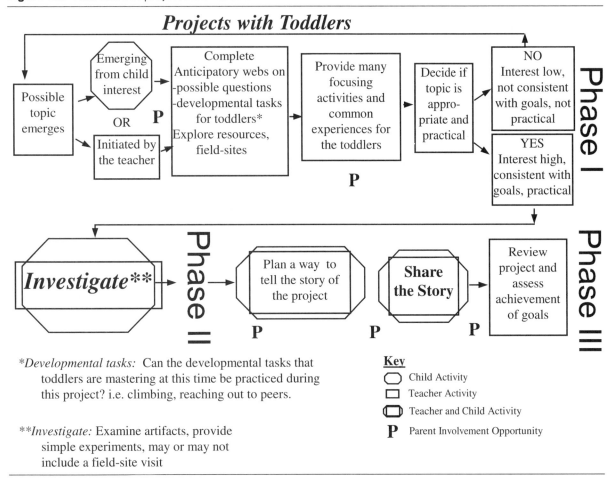

Developmental tasks: Can the developmental tasks that
toddlers are mastering at this time be practiced during
this project? i.e. climbing, reaching out to peers.

Key
○ Child Activity
□ Teacher Activity
▢ Teacher and Child Activity
P Parent Involvement Opportunity

**Investigate:* Examine artifacts, provide
simple experiments, may or may not
include a field-site visit

Figure 6.10 These toddlers in Johnna Gerlach's class at
St. Ambrose Children's Campus place the ball in the pipe
and then watch to see where it comes out.

projects children develop their literacy skills as they use
reading and writing for many purposes. She knows,
however, that learning to do projects with young children is a challenge.

Sometimes teachers have difficulty transitioning
from their instructional plan to truly following the
child's lead and letting them determine the
direction the study will go. Recognizing children's
interest and going with them in that direction can
be a challenge. Teachers have to learn to be
supporters, to scaffold children's learning—
knowing when to step in and support and when
to remain an observer.

Some of the ways teachers can be supported in their
learning is by providing professional development
courses and workshops on the project approach onsite,
providing mentor teachers for teachers new to projects,
and encouraging small groups of teachers to meet for
sharing and dialogue. It is very helpful for teachers if
principals and center directors participate in project

approach training with their staff so they can more fully understand the strategies and the benefits to the children. Cathy Wiggers, like many directors and principals, makes a point of visiting classrooms during work time to see the projects and listen to children talk about their work. Providing planning time for developing projects is also important. Teachers need time to plan together and discuss the projects going on in their classrooms. Administrators can also provide support by assuring that field trips can be taken when needed for investigation, video equipment is available for use, and teachers have cameras and film. Administrators can also set up systems in which teachers can obtain supplies quickly as the project evolves.

Taking the time to support teachers and projects has many beneficial results. These are changes that Ms. Wiggers, as an administrator, has noted:

> When teachers learn to do projects they do more of an in-depth analysis of the learning that is taking place in their classroom. When they see the higher level thinking their children are doing, they raise their expectations for their children. I've seen more sharing and discussion with colleagues as teachers problem-solve and study together how

to reach higher levels of learning in their classroom. This affects their teaching in a positive way. Teachers ponder more deeply how they support children and their learning. They have a greater passion for how children learn.

LEARNING AS A JOURNEY

As presented in Chapter 1, the project approach is not a complete curriculum. It is an approach that constitutes one part of a curriculum for young children. One meaning of the word *approach* is "to come nearer to." Many of the teachers in this book who have integrated projects into their classroom talk about how "they are working on it" or they "aren't there yet," how they are coming closer to their vision of how children can learn and how a project can be an engaged learning experience. They describe the process of learning to do projects as a journey, one they think won't end soon but a journey they are enjoying.

In the last chapter, the reader will join Pam Scranton and her prekindergarten children in Eureka, Illinois, as they take a children's journey of investigation, the Fire Truck Project.

CHAPTER 7

The Fire Truck Project

The Fire Truck Project took place in Bright Beginnings, a prekindergarten program for children at risk funded by the state of Illinois. Under the supervision of Woodford County Special Education Association, the program is in Eureka, Illinois, a small rural community. While all the families in the program live in small towns or more rural environments, they include a range of income levels. Pam Scranton is the teacher, and her aide is Brenda Wiles. Together they work with 18 3- and 4-year-olds. Children with special needs are fully included in the classroom. At the time of this project, the classroom included one child with special needs. The children participate four days a week in a half-day program. On the fifth day Ms. Scranton makes home visits, participates in in-service training, and attends to planning. Ms. Scranton had been guiding projects with children for four years before the project described in this chapter. She had also participated in a study group focused on children's representation in project work, and had experimented with a variety of forms of documentation. The Fire Truck Project, however, was her first project in this school and, more important, this was the first project for her children and their parents.

The project was documented in two ways: by using the Project Planning Journal that is included at the end of the book, and by videotapes made by the teaching staff as well as by some of parents of children in the classroom. Ms. Scranton's videotape and her journal were used to study the progress of the project. A timeline was prepared to study how and when various children participated in the Fire Truck Project. The timeline, which tracks the story of this project, is shown at the top of the pages in the chapter.

When it was decided to use Ms. Scranton's documentation to make a video to show other teachers, a film crew from STARnet at Western Illinois University came to the class at Bright Beginnings to tape additional footage of the fire truck and of the classroom. Ms. Scranton also gave a videotaped interview about the project. The video, *A Children's Journey: Investigating the Fire Truck*

(Illinois STARnet, 2000), is the result of combining these forms of documentation (it is available from Teachers College Press).

The Fire Truck Project was initiated by the children and is a good example of how a project can begin with a catalytic event. The documentation shows how a simple project progresses in a prekindergarten classroom. The following pages are a summary of Ms. Scranton's own words as she discussed the Fire Truck Project, accompanied by our comments, which are included in brackets.

THE CHILDREN'S JOURNEY

Phase I: Getting Started

Day 1: Experiencing the catalytic event

It started when we went on a walk and the children saw a fire truck parked in the street near the school. The children began to talk excitedly, to point, and to ask questions. Some children just stopped walking and stared. One of the firefighters was kind enough to come over to our children and answer their questions. They were very excited and wanted to know "What's that? What's that? What's that button for? Can I try on your boots? Can I try on your hat?" Returning to the classroom, the children continued to be energized by the experience and talked to each other about what they had seen and their own experiences with fire trucks. They were so excited that I began to think "we might have a project here." I asked them if they wanted to know more about the fire truck and if they would like to go see a fire truck and they said, "Yes, teacher let's go see a fire truck!"

This was the very first project for these children. It occurred after we had been in school for about a month. [The children were comfortable in the school environment and knew their classmates fairly well.] One of my goals for the children in this first project was for them to form their own questions and then to ask their own questions. I wanted them to take initiative in their own investigation. I also wanted to start exposing them to representational activities. I wanted them to be able to come back to the classroom after we had a field experience and organize what they had learned. I wanted them to be able to record their information and to represent [draw, construct, paint] what they had learned. I wanted them to be able to represent as they continued to learn new things throughout the project. I guess representation and getting the children to the point where they could think about their own learning were my biggest goals for this first project.

The very first thing we did after we decided "yes, this is what we want to do" was to sit down and initiate two different activities to get the project going. First was accessing their prior knowledge by listing what they knew about fire trucks. The second thing we did was to create a web about what they wanted to know, what they wanted to learn about the fire truck.

We got out a big piece of chart paper and I asked them, "What do you already know about a fire truck?" I wanted to assess their prior knowledge, trying to get an idea about where we were starting from. The children said everything they knew about a fire truck and I put it on the chart paper [Ms. Scranton chose to document what children know by making a list of their statements (see Figure 7.1). She could have chosen to create a web, but the children's ideas were offered quickly. She didn't think that she needed a graphic organizer to stimulate thought.]

Then, later that same day, I sat down with a small group of the most interested children. This time I did some webbing. I put the fire station in the middle of the web. The children made me change it. I wrote fire station at first because, in my mind, that was where we were going to go: to the fire station. Then one of the children said "No, no, teacher! Fire truck! We want to know about fire truck."

At that point I thought to myself that they were guiding their learning. They didn't want to know what happens in a fire station; they wanted to know about the fire truck. So, I wrote the words *fire truck* down and then we started talking.

"So, what do you want to know? What are we going to do when we get there? What questions are you going to ask the firefighter? What are you wondering about?"

I could not write fast enough to get down all of their questions. They had so many things listed on that web and it just took all I could do to keep up with them (see Figure 7.2). I was writing very quickly, and the children were taking turns back and forth. It was the first time since we started school that I saw them really talking to each other instead of talking at each other. Jordan

Figure 7.1 Ms. Scranton writes down children's thoughts about the fire truck.

brought up the fact that he wanted to see that "thing that winds the hoses up." Evan said, "You mean the steering wheel," and Jordan said, "No, that thing that winds the hoses up."

Jordan knew what he meant; Evan didn't know what he meant. They were talking back and forth instead of directing their questions at me. I was pleased with that first webbing experience. It was the first time I had asked them to think about what they wanted to learn.

[This project, like many projects that begin with catalytic events, progressed quickly through the first phase. The teacher was not obliged to spend extensive time getting the young investigators to focus on the topic because they were already focused. Nor was there a need to build a common experience regarding the topic because everyone had the experience of seeing the fire truck at the same time. It was also a highly motivating experience and the memory of the experience was vivid. The children also had a common reference for vocabulary related to the fire truck.]

Day 2: Clarifying the questions

The next day I brought in some books with photographs of fire trucks. I brought in these books to stimulate the children's vocabulary and to stimulate their thinking. The books were very helpful. I wanted to just give them a jumping-off point to start our conversation. [Ms. Scranton frequently uses the strategy of having photos, books, or pictures related to the topic to start the discussion with 3- and 4-year-olds. It revives young investigators' memories of experiences they have with a topic. It also enables children who have a limited vocabulary related to the topic or who are not verbal to indicate

Fire Truck Project Days 1–5

Day 1	Day 2	Day 3	Day 4	Day 5
Catalytic event: Children see fire truck	Clarifying: "What We Want to Know"	Field-site visited	Talked about trip Talked about representation	
Made list "What We Know" "What We Want to Know"	Questions webbed	Questions answered	Began construction of fire truck	

Phase One		**Phase Two**		

what interests them. Ms. Scranton focused the conversation on the questions for investigation.]

I said, "Oh, look, there are the ladders. Do we want to know about ladders? I wonder how many ladders there are on a fire truck?" [Forming questions was modeled by the teacher when she shared a few questions of her own. The children had no difficulty generating questions.] One of the most interesting questions was whether you had to be an engineer to drive a fire truck. So we put that question down on our web. "Do you have to be an engineer to drive a fire truck?" They wanted to know how fast the fire truck can go. "How

Figure 7.2 These are the questions that the children generated and Ms. Scranton recorded on a web.

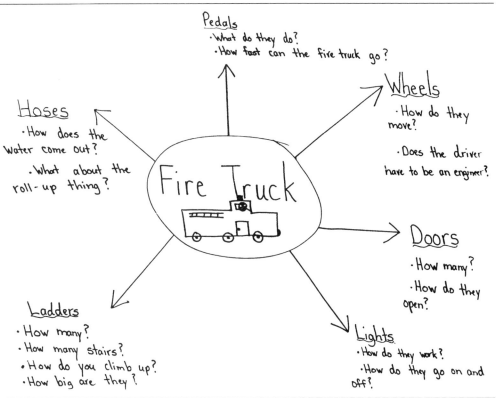

fast can the fire truck go?" They wanted to know about the lights. "What makes the lights come on?" They wanted to know about those sirens. They wanted to know about the different materials on the truck: the items, the ladders, and the axes. They used a lot of phrases like, "you know, that thing." They didn't have the vocabulary yet because we hadn't been on the field experience.

They wanted to know whether, if the fire truck went too fast, the policeman would arrest the firefighter. That surprised me. Our playground is situated on the main road, and we see emergency vehicles as they go out on calls. Several times we watched ambulances and fire trucks go by very fast. The children had seen how fast they go.

They wanted to know about the firefighter. They wanted to know where the firefighter ate all his dinners. That was one of the questions: "Does he eat all his dinners at the fire station? Does the firefighter have kids?"

[Once the list of questions for investigation was completed, the project moved into Phase II.]

Phase II: Investigating

Day 3: Visiting the field-site

We prepared children by talking with them about the experience. We talked about who would want to do what. Then, before the actual field experience, Ms. Wiles and I divided the children into two groups. The project group was responsible for gathering the information, asking the questions, recording answers, and doing the field sketches. The other group was to be involved with more manipulative kinds of activities like trying the firefighter gear on and climbing on the fire truck. [All children participated in the project. The project group, as Ms. Scranton referred to them, was comprised of children who were the most interested in the questions. This group consisted mainly of older 3-year-olds and 4-year-olds. The other group was composed mainly of the younger 3-year-olds.]

[While preparing the children for the experience,] I talked to the children about how there would be two groups and who would be in what group.

We sat down [with the project group] and talked [about the questions] before we went on the field experience. We decided together what questions each child wanted to ask the firefighters. We wrote the questions with illustrations on little 3" × 5" cards that we clipped to their clipboards. They also had paper [on their clipboards on which to make] their field sketches. They had to decide for themselves which question they wanted to answer. Then each child was responsible when we got to the field experience for asking that question, with adult help. We had parent volunteers who were help-

ing the children do that. The children were also responsible for making sure that the answer, the firefighter's answer, was recorded on their clipboard . . . on the card or on the paper. [Ms. Scranton stressed the two tasks: remembering the question and recording the answer.] In this project the investigating and answering of questions happened on the field experience. [In many projects, the investigation may include additional field-site visits and additional visiting experts. The investigation on this first simple project focused on the visit to the fire truck at the fire station. Because of the videotaping, the children were able to review and revisit the fire truck many times.]

The fire station is really close to our classroom so we walked. Besides my associate teacher and myself, we had parent volunteers who went with us. When we got there, we divided the children into the two groups. [Ms. Scranton took responsibility for the project group and her associate teacher for the younger group.] Ms. Wiles's group [with their parent helpers] went off to explore the fire truck, and my group sat down with our expert for the day, the firefighter, who answered the children's questions. The children were responsible for asking the question that was on their 3" × 5" cards. They were responsible, with adult help, for recording the answer, either by writing the answer or by drawing a sketch of the firefighter's (the expert's) answer to their question.

The project group also sketched the fire truck. They graphed the materials that they were wondering about on the fire truck. They graphed how many ladders there were, how many hoses there were, how many windows there were on a fire truck. The graphing part of the field experience went really well. This was the children's first experience with the tally graph. We had graphed several times before doing a picture graph and a bar graph, but this was the first time they'd used tally graphs. The children spent at least 10 or 15 minutes graphing the parts of the fire truck that they had asked about on their web. I had made a graph for them with a picture of a tire and a column for them to make their tally marks, and a picture of the windows, and so forth. They could take the clipboards and just walk around the fire truck and mark their tally sheets, and count [see Figure 7.3]. One of the firefighters took down the ladders so they could count the ladders individually because there are lots of ladders on a fire truck! They for the most part were very successful. They really enjoyed the counting as the numbers got higher and higher. "There are eight windows on this fire truck!" They were amazed! They started to count the hoses. The firefighter said, "Oh, I'm going to have to bring them down. There are a lot of hoses on this fire truck!" As their counting grew they just got more and more excited about putting those tally marks [on the paper] the right way.

Figure 7.3 The children use tally marks to record numerical data.

[One of Ms. Scranton's curriculum goals is for the children to use one-to-one correspondence to solve problems. At the 4-year-old level, children may match each cup to a plate so there is an equal number of plates and cups. At the 5-year-old level children begin to use one-to-one correspondence when pointing to and assigning a number to each object in a group (Jablon, Marsden, Meisels, & Dichtelmiller, 1994)].

That was also something I collected for their work-sampling portfolios because it showed their use of one-to-one correspondence. A lot of my Work Sampling comes out of the project work. [The Work Sampling System (Meisels et al., 1994) is an authentic assessment system that Ms. Scranton uses to document children's learning. It consists of a developmental checklist and a portfolio; see Chapter 6.]

The field sketching was hard at first because I had asked them to sit down in front of the fire truck with this blank piece of paper and this clipboard [see Figure 7.4]. The fire truck was so big and so daunting to them that they had trouble at first. [Ms. Scranton asked the children to sit on the floor by the fire truck to draw. She focused the children's attention on the parts of the fire truck and coached them in how to begin drawing. Her approach to the task was similar to that recommended in Chapter 4.]

It was really hard for them to represent what they were seeing on this big blank piece of paper because that fire truck had so many things on it. I heard a lot of "I can't do it teacher." "I can't draw this fire truck, it's too big." "There are too many things." "There are too many ladders on the fire truck." So I had to sit down and we had to talk about drawing the fire truck. I had to point out things. I had to break it down for them at first because this was their first field sketching experience. [It is sometimes difficult for children to make their first

field sketch. This teacher recognized that some of the children were having this problem. This is how she got them started.]

So we sat down and I said "Okay, let's talk about the fire truck. Let's talk about something that's really big [on the fire truck] that you can draw." They looked around and my eyes just went to the tires and I thought, "Okay, I know they can do the tires. The tires are on the bottom of the fire truck. Maybe if I focused them there they can build on that for their sketch." So that's what we started with. I said to them, "Go stand by those tires. Look how big they are. Look how many tires there are. I bet you can draw those tires. I bet you can put those tires on your paper." They could. That was something they knew they could do. They could draw a round tire and they could count how many were on the fire truck. They knew, sitting right next to it, how big they were. So that made them feel successful.

After that we just went on. I said, "Okay, what about the fire truck itself; what shape is it? Is it a circle like

Figure 7.4 The children are drawing as they observe the fire truck from different angles.

the tire?" "No, no teacher it's not a circle." "Well what do you think? What shape, what could we use to draw the actual fire truck part?" It just seemed to flow from there. It just seemed like those very first pencil marks, the making of those tires, got them started. It wasn't [didn't appear to be] so hard after that. But staring at that big fire truck with all those things on it was really daunting for them at first.

I think teacher coaching is a vital part of project work and a vital part of representation. It is the teacher's responsibility to support the children, to scaffold them as they are learning to represent [what they are observing]. My just sitting there with them and helping them break that fire truck down so it wasn't so big and it wasn't so daunting helped them get past that initial "I can't do it. I can't draw this fire truck."

Meanwhile, Ms. Wiles's group was doing thematic play. The children in this group were younger. They weren't at the stage of representing their learning on paper. Trying on the firefighter's gear and putting the hat on were their ways of investigating. They were involved in climbing on the fire truck and sitting in the driver's seat and pretending to drive.

My group got to do that too, but they did it after they had conducted their investigations and asked their questions. At first it was kind of hard, because the project group was sitting by the fire truck trying to do these things listening to the firefighter and the other group was climbing all over the fire truck. They were getting up there and turning the steering wheel and opening the doors and pushing the buttons. My children were looking around. I had to talk with them about how they were doing important work because they were finding out the answers to the questions the class had wanted to know. I also told them they would do that [get to climb, play, etc.] later. Then I moved them around so the other group wasn't quite so noticeable and started doing the sketching and graphing. That worked.

After they recorded their information, made their field sketches, and finished graphing, the children got into the truck. The firefighter let them crawl inside and sit in the driver's seat. They turned the steering wheel. One of our little boys, Gavin, got to turn on the sirens and flip on the lights. Two or three of them got to be up [in the cab] at a time. As they were up there you could see their eyes and their wonder at all those buttons and all those levers. They had lots of questions: "What does this button do? What does this lever do?" The firefighter, the expert, was just wonderful about patiently answering their questions and letting them manipulate the buttons and the levers, always making sure that what they were touching was safe for them to be touching. He was really good about

letting the children manipulate the parts of the fire truck, letting them find out what it felt like to be sitting high up in this driver's seat. "How high up are you, Gavin, when you look down in that window? Can you see me down here waving at you?" The children were physically feeling what it is like to be in that fire truck.

Day 4: Reviewing and revisiting the experience

Deciding to build a fire truck

Beginning construction

The day after the field trip the children came back to the classroom. The night before I had brought in a refrigerator box that I had been saving for a project, hoping that they would want to construct with it. I set this big refrigerator box in the middle of our art center, moved away the chairs, moved away the table, and just set this box in the middle. The children came in just full of "remember this, remember this"—just full of remembering what they had seen the previous day. The minute they walked in and were hanging up their coats they asked, "What's the box for? What are we going to do with the box?" I said to them, "I am wondering what you might want to do with the box. Be thinking about what you could do with the box. I am wondering if you have any ideas."

I was hoping that the children would say "We can build a fire truck." I was hoping they would get around to the point where they would look at that box and say, "Look at that box over there, we can build that fire truck!" but they never really did. I was hoping they would transfer all that they were talking about and all that they had experienced the day before into a representation with that box. They never really got to that point on their own. So I had to steer them in that direction. I said something like, "You guys have so much information about a fire truck; you really learned a lot yesterday. You know where the lever water buttons go, you know where the button goes to turn on the siren. You know where the ax goes on the fire truck. I think you could build a fire truck." That's all it took—"I wonder if you could build a fire truck."

"Oh, yeah, we can build a fire truck! We can make buttons and we can make a lever!" Just answer after answer came. We can do this and we can do this. I could barely rein them in. All it took from me was one question, "I wonder if you could build a fire truck." And right away they started thinking, "We can do that, we're smart and we know where those things go."

After that we broke up the group for our learning center time. A group of children had decided to construct the fire truck, and they went to the art center and got right to it. They got the janitor, who had a big razor blade knife. The children told him, "Here's where we want the windows. Here's where we want the door. Here's where we want the windshield." He cut it for them. They cut it that day and began painting it.

Days 5–6: Painting the fire truck

Gathering resources

The children used the materials that they had worked on during the field-site visit, their field sketches, for resources. They also used the books that we had looked at when we made our list of questions. We read the stories during morning group time, and we used the books during small-group time. We opened the pages when the children wanted to know something—for example, we tried to find what Jordan was talking about that winds the hoses, but we couldn't find it.

Day 7: Painting the tires

Revisiting the field experience through video

Beginning dashboard construction

We used the video to revisit and gain more information as the children were constructing the fire truck. [Ms. Scranton utilized the video of the site visit not just as a documentation tool but as a resource for children to use. The video enabled the children to relive the experience of the field-site visit. Footage of the fire truck and its parts, without children, allowed the children to concentrate on looking at the details on the truck. This process of using video and audio recordings or photographs of field-sites captures the site so children can study the site and artifacts more closely in their classroom.]

[On the video] the children saw the buttons on the dashboard and started to gather the junk for making the dashboard. The next day they started bringing things from home. They said, "This could be the button for the siren." "This button is for the lights." They brought cork and bottlecaps and buttons and spray can lids. They just took off. After that, all I had to do was stand back to make sure that I had enough glue and the paint they needed. [See Figure 7.5. An interesting thing about this first project is how the children took responsibility very early for bringing in materials. This is an indication that they continued to think about the project when they were away from the school. Items were brought in for a specific purpose, not just scrap materials for any use, but an item that would represent a specific button on

Figure 7.5 A 4-year-old uses bottle caps to represent the buttons and levers he observed on the fire truck's dashboard.

the fire truck. This process went on from Day 7 through Day 13, or 7 school days, almost 2 weeks in a 4-day-preschool program.]

Days 8–9: Adding the steering wheel

Continuing dashboard construction

The children remembered the steering wheel when they reviewed the video. So the next two days two children worked on the steering wheel.

Day 9: Beginning the lights/sirens

Continuing dashboard construction

[A group of girls remembered the lights and the sirens and decided to make these.] Ashley and Katie were designing the siren and the lights that went on the top of the fire truck. They took on this job. It caused a lively discussion. [As is often the case in projects with young investigators, the construction becomes the location of many problem-solving sequences, both construction problems and social problems.]

David and Evan were working inside on all these buttons and levers [and the girls were working on the outside]. The boys got into a very lively discussion with Ashley that all her lights were wrong. She had taken a Kleenex box and painted it and glued it up on top for the lights. David at one point stuck his head out and said, "That is wrong, Ashley." Evan said, "Yeah, they don't look like that. The lights don't look like that. They are shiny." So the two girls and two boys got into a discussion about these lights. I was holding the video camera recording them while they were discussing this. As a teacher, that was hard for me. Sometimes you want to step in there and say, "Now David, you need to use your nice words with Ashley." But as a person who does projects with children, I knew I had to just step back and let them talk that out. That is a valuable part of doing projects. Projects encourage children to listen to each other, to listen to each other's thoughts. Children listen to each other's ideas and learn to compromise. They have to work together to construct something. So I didn't intervene even though they were getting pretty lively, and there was some arguing going on. The girls gave in. The girls took their lights back off. They went over and they found some paper that they thought was shiny. David and Evan came back out, and they said, "That's not right, those don't look right either."

That was the end of that work time, and we went away that day with no lights for the fire truck, and the girls feeling pretty mad at David and Evan for not liking their lights.

Day 10: Solving the problem of the lights

Continuing dashboard construction

Beginning the ladders

But the very next day, David came in with some aluminum pie tins, new shiny aluminum pie tins. The boys took them over to Ashley and Katie in group time before we started our morning group activities and said, "These would make good lights." Ashley looked at them and said, "Yeah, these are good! They're shiny! They'll make good lights."

So that day the girls went back to the lights. They first tried painting them. Well, the paint didn't stick to the aluminum pie tin. They wanted them to be red and blue like the lights they had seen on the field experience. The paint wasn't working. As soon as it dried it chipped off.

They revisited the video. They figured they could cut out paper, construction paper in the color that they wanted, the blue and red, and they could glue it inside the pie tin. [see Figure 7.6] So they had the shininess and they had the color that they wanted for the lights. Gavin also revisited the video and remembered the ladders. He began to work on making ladders.

Day 11: Attaching the lights

Continuing dashboard construction

So the girls now were at the point where they had to fasten those lights on the fire truck. They tried glue at first. The glue didn't work. The pie tins fell right off.

Figure 7.6 Ashley and Katie try out the pie tins that David brought for the fire truck headlights.

I had some great big wide clear tape that the boys were using to fasten some of their levers onto the inside of the fire truck. Ashley found that tape and figured out that she could tape the back of those aluminum pie tins to the truck. That satisfied them, and the lights were on the fire truck.

Day 12: Completing the ladders

Continuing dashboard construction

Gavin continued to work on trying to make ladders. He tried a number of items from construction paper to blocks, but on Day 12 settled into making his ladder out of toilet paper rolls and gift-wrap tubes, which he taped together.

Day 13: Continuing dashboard construction

Involving all the children

The children who chose not to be involved in construction were still involved in the project. There is a lot of literature about fire trucks, and we shared many good books with the children. Firefighters had given us some of their equipment and the children explored these [items]. We put props in the dramatic play area, including hats and firefighter coats. There was a lot of dramatic play. The children would line up the chairs for a fire truck. We made sure that we had the colors of the fire truck on the paint easel and in the art area. We put up children's sketches and work on display. The children who were working on the fire truck reported back to the group what they were doing. Everyone watched the progress of the fire truck. There were many activities [songs, fingerplays, stories] that related to the fire

Fire Truck Project Days 6–10

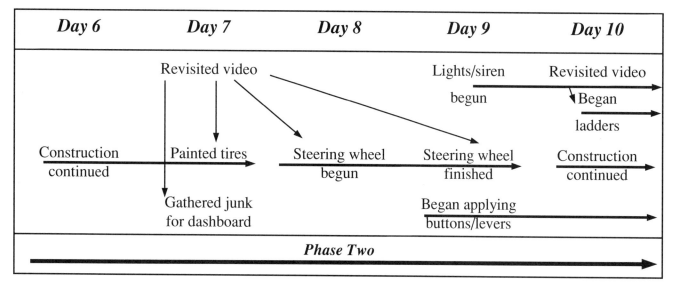

truck, which were done with the group or as optional activities.

Day 14: Completing dashboard construction

Day 15: Revisiting the video

     Adding hoses

     Beginning the ax

[When the dashboard was completed, there was a discussion of whether the fire truck was finished. The children decided to look at the video again. They saw and quickly added the hoses. One child saw the ax and began working on an ax.]

Days 16–18: Completing the ax

     Pronouncing the fire truck finished

When that group of constructors—the children who were constructing the fire truck—felt that they had finished their work, we put the fire truck in the middle of our large play area, the block area. This is an area that can take a lot of movement and action. The children who were constructing the fire truck were ready to play. They got in there on the first day and they really played, some really good play. They put on the fire hats, played going to the fires. But this play didn't last very long, although I thought that these children who had spent so many weeks constructing this fire truck would just play forever in it. They only really played for 2 days. Then

they were done. You could just tell that they had finished with this part of their representation of the learning experience. That is when that group moved to discussion and the mural work.

Day 19: Beginning younger children's play
     with construction

Those younger 3-year-olds who were not involved with the representational part of the project looked at this fire truck that was now empty, and you could just see in their eyes, "Yes, it's our turn!" They got in there, and this incredible play started happening with these 3-year-olds in the fire truck. As I was thinking about that I was wondering. I would really have thought those children who constructed the fire truck who had claimed so much ownership and worked on it for so many weeks would be the ones to play in it. It was really puzzling to me at first why these children were done and their "fire was out." They were moving on to something else, and these 3s came in and were doing these incredible play sequences in the fire truck. I have gotten to the point in my thinking where I feel this is the way those 3-year-olds are representing what they know at their stage of development. They are not to the point in their development where they can sketch or graph or construct their learning in that way. But they know what happens on a fire truck. They saw what happens on the field experience. They know what a firefighter looks like. They saw him put on his gear. They know what a fire truck sounds like when the sirens go and the lights

Fire Truck Project Days 11–15

Day 11	*Day 12*	*Day 13*	*Day 14*	*Day 15*

Lights attached →

Ladders
completed →

Revisited video ↓

Construction ———————————————————————————→   Hoses added
continued   Ax is begun

Buttons/levers ————————————————————————   Dashboard
applied   construction ends

Phase Two ——————————————————————————————————————→

---

go on. They represented that learning through their play.

Day 20: Attempting to redraw sketches

   Continuing younger children's
   dramatic play

[As the older children became less consumed with the construction of the fire truck and appeared to have satisfied their desire to play in the construction, their teacher focused them back on their drawings.] After they felt finished with the fire truck and play had begun on the fire truck by the other children, that's when their [the constructors'] interests turned to looking at their field sketches. We took their field sketches back out, and we sat down in a small group, and I gave them new pieces of paper. And I said, "You know, now that you've been to the fire truck, now that you've built the fire truck, you've figured out where the buttons go, you've figured out how the ladder hangs on the fire truck, let's draw this fire truck again. Let's think about this fire truck again and draw it on a new piece of paper."

That day didn't go very well. They looked at that blank piece of paper and their old field sketches, and they reproduced exactly what they had done on that field sketch. So I thought to myself, "What am I not doing? What am I not giving them? What am I not scaffolding for them that they cannot think about the fire truck and think about how they would change it?"

Days 21–23: Revisiting the video

   Redrawing field sketches

   Continuing dramatic play

So the next day, when we tried this again, I did it in a small group again. Except this time I took them away from the table, we got clipboards, we sat down on our rug, and we watched the video of the fire truck again. I would pause it and fast forward it to the parts they wanted to see again, and I would rewind it. That seemed to stimulate them, and they would point out and yell, "Oh, yeah, there are the ladders! There, there . . . there's the ax over there! It's on the back. Oh, remember it said 'fire truck.'"

That was the first time they had really picked out any letters on the fire truck. Those letters were then seen on their second and third redraws. On their field sketches there were no letters. But they did . . . after watching the video and looking at that fire truck more closely. They were able to draw their second and third sketches of the fire truck, from watching the video [see Figure 7.7].

Days 24 and 25: Beginning the mural

   Continuing dramatic play

The mural was another way that the children represented what they knew about the fire truck. They took their field sketches that they were working on and brought them over to the art center with a great big

Fire Truck Project Days 16–20

Day 16	*Day 17*	*Day 18*	*Day 19*	*Day 20*
		Play by constructors began ⟶	Play by constructors ended	Constructors attempted to draw fire truck
Ax completed ⟶		Construction completed		
			Play began by younger group children ⟶	
Phase Two ⟶				

piece of paper. We talked about how you could put the fire truck onto this great big piece of paper. Two children were the most interested in working on this. I asked them, "Do you want to change something about the fire truck on your sketches before you put it on this big piece of paper?" Yes, they wanted to do the sketches again, so I got some clean sheets of paper, and they sketched what they wanted the mural to look like. The next day they came back [to the art area] ready to put these images on the big piece of paper. That is a pretty high level of skill for 3- and 4-year-olds. A large piece of mural paper is also very daunting [like the paper and the fire truck]. They have to figure how to spatially orga-

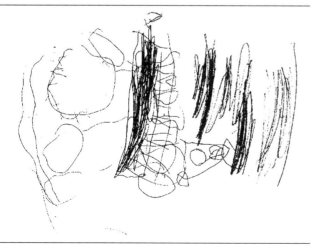

Figure 7.7 David's second sketch, which he did 17 days after the first, shows the growth in his knowledge about the fire truck.

nize this fire truck on this large sheet of mural paper. There was a lot of discussion, especially between Ashley and Gavin, about where to put the front of the fire truck, and how big the ladders should be. The ladders were very important to Gavin, because he had constructed the actual ladders on the fire truck. It was very important to Gavin that these got constructed the right way on the fire truck and then on the mural. As they were working they were really talking to each other. I was taking down what they were saying to each other. Later I displayed [this documentation] with their mural. It gives someone viewing the mural real insight into what those children were thinking. What are the thought processes they had to go through to get that fire truck on that large piece of mural paper? [see Figure 7.8.]

Day 26: Finishing the mural

Continuing dramatic play

Phase III: Concluding the Project

Day 27: Talking about how to share what was learned

Continuing dramatic play

As the play started to wind down, children were getting into different interests. It was December, and we were beginning candlemaking. I could tell that the interest in the project was really waning; the interest in the fire truck just wasn't there anymore. I sat down with the group, and I asked them, "You have learned so much about the fire truck, how are you going to share that learning? How are we going to share what we know

Fire Truck Project Days 21–25

Day 21	*Day 22*	*Day 23*	*Day 24*	*Day 25*

Revisited video

Redrew sketches

Mural begun →

Play continued by
younger children →

Phase Two →

about the fire truck with other boys and girls or with moms and dads? Do you have some ideas about what we could do?" They did, so we took out another big sheet of paper, and we listed their ideas. Someone said we could make a book. Someone else said we could do a play about the fire truck. Someone said, "Let's make a movie about the fire truck." That idea was a hit and everyone voted to make a movie.

Figure 7.8 The mural of the white fire truck shows that the children know many of the parts of the fire truck, where they are located, and how to read and write the words "fire truck."

Day 28: Planning the movie

          Continuing dramatic play

The next day we met again, and I asked them, "Okay, you are going to make a movie. Who is going to do the talking in the movie? Who's going to talk about the hoses? Who is going to talk about the ladders?" They had to decide. So this group talked, and one child became sort of the leader and he said, "Evan, you should do the buttons. Gavin, you should do the ladder because you made the ladder." They talked about what they would say. I talked about the kind of voice they would have to use—a little bit louder voice.

Day 29: Making the movie

          Continuing dramatic play

We made the movie during small-group time. We put the fire truck back in position, and the children decided who would go first and they made a movie [see Figure 7.9]. [The children decided the order of the speaking parts for the movie.]

Day 30: Celebrating at the movie party

The day after that we invited boys and girls from the other class, and we popped popcorn, and they came and watched our movie. [Ms. Scranton also shared the Fire Truck Project with parents through a wall display and a project history book.]

Fire Truck Project Days 26–40

Day 26	*Day 27*	*Day 28*	*Day 29*	*Day 30-40*
	Children discuss how to share story of the project ↓			
Mural →	Decided to	Movie	Movie	Movie Party
finished	make movie	planned	produced	Day 30
Play continued by				Play continues
younger children				until Day 40
				Project ends
Phase Two →	*Phase Three* →			

Days 30–39: Continuing dramatic play

[Dramatic play by the young children who were not constructing continued for 21 days. There were variations in play scenarios, and children floated in and out of the play sequences but play continued to be purposeful and highly engaging.]

Day 40: Terminating the project

[Ms. Scranton's class was moved to a new building over the holiday break. Children were still playing in the fire truck. By this time the cardboard fire truck was pretty dilapidated from the extensive and vigorous dramatic play. It also occupied a significant part of the play area of the room. The teacher talked to the children, and they decided that the fire truck would be left behind. This terminated the project and ended the journey.]

Looking Back on the Journey

This was the first project of this prekindergarten class. They went on to do another project about the veterinarian, that same year. A summary of this project is in Chapter 1. In other parts of this book, Ms. Scranton shares her thoughts on how the children and parents responded to this subsequent project. Children who were 3 years old at the time of the Fire Truck Project continued with the same teacher the next year. These children became project leaders and were enthusiastic young investigators.

Ms. Scranton shared her video of the Fire Truck Project and her documentation with her new colleagues and the administrators of her program. Response to the project was so enthusiastic that all teachers participated in a project approach class the following year and are currently in their second year of doing projects with children. In addition to teachers in early childhood, teachers of children with special needs at other age levels also participated. Ms. Scranton's class this year has three children with special needs fully included. She and her young investigators are currently in the middle of a new journey, the investigation of acorns. She continues to involve all of her children in the projects and thinks all children have much to gain from projects.

Figure 7.9 Children who worked on the construction of the fire truck explained what they did and why on the video they made for the party.

CLOSING THOUGHTS

Many of the projects referred to throughout this book might prompt readers to ask why the time and energy devoted to them were warranted, given the topics under investigation. After all, very little of the knowledge gained in projects at the preschool, kindergarten, and first-grade level could not be "picked up" by most children as they grow to adolescence: Sooner or later most individuals acquire as much knowledge of the nature of fire trucks or turtles or the work of a veterinarian as they need for competence in their daily lives. So, we could ask: Why bother? These topics can hardly be thought of as "core knowledge" required by the children for full participation in the mainstream culture. However, close reading of the Fire Truck Project and viewing of the video of that project (Illinois STARnet, 2000) suggest a number of answers to that question.

First, most of the important inborn intellectual dispositions are expressed and thereby strengthened through this project, rather than ignored or set aside by excessive emphasis on rote learning, drill, and exercises. The disposition to observe and to formulate questions to be answered was strengthened by the investigation of what was to the children an interesting phenomenon. When the teacher invites children to predict what the answers to their questions are likely to be, their dispositions to hypothesize are expressed; when the teacher encourages them to share the bases of their predictions, their dispositions to reflect on their own hunches are expressed. When children return to the class and compare their findings with their predictions, their dispositions to check the facts, to be empirical, can be developed. The list of these kinds of learnings is potentially very long, and they are all "life skills" not usually included on school district or state tests.

Second, looking at the ability of such young children to engage in their first experience of representing numbers through tallying and graphing parts of an object of real interest to them, we can easily recognize how this can help them understand the representational function of mathematical symbols and the purposes they can serve. In this context, mathematical operations are intellectual engagements rather than rote learning or counting for the sake of reciting numbers from 1 to 10 as in many academically oriented curricula.

Third, considering the part of the Fire Truck Project in which David and Evan criticized Ashley's and Katie's first attempt at painting the lights for the truck, we can see that they were learning another life skill not on any standardized performance test: They were learning to accept criticism. Indeed, it is most likely that deep down, they agreed with their critics. We often underestimate young children's capacities to assess the qual-

ity of their efforts. If adults always intervene to soften such exchanges—and the teacher admitted that it was tempting to intervene and soften the criticism—the children may learn that criticism is damaging rather than often instructive. They may learn to feel sorry for themselves, rather than to attend to the problem to be solved— learning of value throughout life. Notice that when their critic offered the aluminum pie tins, they agreed that those would "make good lights."

Throughout projects like this one, a variety of social skills are called on as the work progresses, and the children exchange ideas and opinions; share responsibility for posing questions to experts; offer each other suggestions and corrections, as well as encouragement to try something again. All of these occur during genuine encounters about something that matters to them. There are many more examples of intellectual and social dispositions and competencies, as well as academic skills that are strengthened during good project work.

We want to emphasize the central issue of the quality of the work undertaken in projects. Like any other classroom procedures or processes, projects can be done well or poorly. Good-quality projects are those focused on worthwhile topics that constitute the content of their work; they involve children in important processes such as setting the research agenda that takes them in depth into the topic and preparing products that are detailed representations of the results of their investigation experiences. Most teachers with whom we have worked indicate that it takes a few project experiences before they develop full confidence in the children's abilities to take initiative and responsibility and to persist in their investigations. Once this confidence is acquired, they become co-investigators in that they are learning from their experiences with the children about how best to provide the environments in which they can flourish and grow. They also report that while the work is intense, it is both interesting and satisfying for the children and for themselves.

This book began with a quote from Ms. Scranton about why she likes to do projects:

> I just love to do projects with children because I think it is exciting watching them construct their own knowledge base . . . watching them decide what interests them the most, investigating it, asking questions about it. I like seeing children excited about what they're doing, excited about their learning.

In studying the project approach in prekindergarten, kindergarten, and first-grade classrooms, we have, above all, been most impressed with this enthusiasm of children, parents, and teachers. In project after project, documentation has captured the energy and the kind of deeply engaged learning experiences that occur in good projects. Teachers seem to become reenergized by watching their young investigators. Many do not just become co-learners with the children, but often embark on their own journeys. By observing, listening, and documenting they become investigators not only of the project topic but of how children learn.

We have seen the project approach change teachers and teaching. As administrator Cathy Wiggers has said, "Learning to do the project approach affects all areas of teaching, not just project work." That is perhaps the greatest benefit of projects, that learning and teaching continue to be adventures for all investigators, young and old alike.

References

The American heritage dictionary (3rd ed.). (1992). Boston: Houghton Mifflin.

Aradema, V. (1993). *The ostrich and crocodile*. New York: Scholastic.

Beneke, S. (1998). *Rearview mirror: A preschool car project*. Champaign, IL: ERIC Clearinghouse on Elementary and Early Childhood Education.

Berk, L. (1991). *Child development*. Boston: Allyn and Bacon.

Berk, L., & Winsler, A. (1995). *Scaffolding children's learning: Vygotsky and early childhood education*. Washington, DC: National Association for the Education of Young Children.

Bodrova, E., & Leong, D. (1996). *Tools of the mind: The Vygotskian approach to early childhood education*. Englewood Cliffs, NJ: Prentice-Hall.

Bredekamp, S., & Rosegrant, T. (1995). *Reaching potentials: Transforming early childhood curriculum and assessment* (Vol. 2). Washington, DC: National Association for the Education of Young Children.

Bryson, E. (1994). *Will a project approach to learning provide children opportunities to do purposeful reading and writing, as well as provide opportunities for authentic learning in other curriculum areas?* Urbana, IL: ERIC Clearinghouse on Elementary and Early Childhood.

Cadwell, L. (1997). *Bringing Reggio Emilia home: An innovative approach to early childhood education*. New York: Teachers College Press.

Carle, E. (1984). *The very hungry caterpillar*. New York: Putnam Publishing.

Catherwood, D. (1999). New views on the young brain: Offerings from developmental psychology to early childhood education. *Contemporary Issues in Early Childhood Education, 1*(1). University College, Worcester, United Kingdom.

Chard, S. C. (1994). *The project approach: A practical guide, I and II*. New York: Scholastic.

Chard, S. C. (1998a). Drawing in the context of a project. In J. H. Helm (Ed.), *The project approach catalog 2* (pp. 1:11–1:12). Champaign, IL: ERIC Clearinghouse on Elementary and Early Childhood Education.

Chard, S. C. (1998b). *Representation and mastering the medium*. Posting July 11, 1998 on Projects-L Listserv, Champaign, IL: ERIC Clearinghouse on Elementary and Early Childhood Education.

Children's Defense Fund. (1998). *Facts about child care in America* [updated July 8, 1998]. Washington, DC: Author.

Christian, D. (1994). *Two way bilingual education: Students learning through two languages*. Santa Cruz, CA: National Center for Research on Cultural Diversity and Second Language Learning.

DeVries, R., Reese-Learned, H., & Morgan, P. (1991). Sociomoral development in direct-instruction, eclectic, and constructivist kindergartens: A study of children's enacted interpersonal understanding. *Early Childhood Research Quarterly, 6*(4), 473–517.

Dodge, D. T., & Colker, L. (1992). *Creative curriculum for early childhood*. Washington, DC: Teaching Strategies.

Donaldson, M. (1978). *Children's minds*. Glasgow: Fontana.

DuCharme, C. (1993, November). *Historical roots of the project approach in the United States: 1850–1930*. Paper presented at the annual meeting of the National Association for the Education of Young Children, Anaheim, CA.

Edmiaston, R. (1998). Projects in inclusive early childhood classrooms. In J. H. Helm (Ed.), *The project approach catalog 2* (pp. 1:19–1:22). Champaign, IL: ERIC Clearinghouse on Elementary and Early Childhood Education.

Edwards, C., Gandini, L., & Forman, G. (Eds.). (1993). *The hundred languages of children: The Reggio approach*. Stamford, CT: Ablex.

Edwards, C., Gandini, L., & Forman, G. (Ed.). (1998). *The hundred languages of children: The Reggio approach— advanced reflections* (2nd ed.). Stamford, CT: Ablex.

Epstein, J. (1995). School/family/community partnerships: Caring for the children we share. *Phi Delta Kappan, 76*(9), 701–712.

Gandini, L. (1993). Fundamentals of the Reggio Emilia approach to early childhood education. *Young Children, 49*, 4–8.

Gandini, L. (1997). Foundations of the Reggio Emilia approach. In J. Hendricks (Ed.), *First steps toward teaching the Reggio way* (pp. 14–25). Upper Saddle River, NJ: Prentice Hall.

Gandini, L., & Edwards, C. D. (2000). *Bambini: The Italian approach to infant/toddler care*. New York: Teachers College Press.

Goal 3 and 4 Technical Planning Group. (1993). *Promises to keep: Creating high standards for American students.* Washington, DC: National Education Goals Panel.

Harlan, J. (1984). *Science experiences for the early childhood years.* Columbus, OH: Merrill.

Heidemann, S., & Hewitt, D. (1992). *Pathways to play: Developing play skills in young children.* St. Paul, MN: Redleaf Press.

Helm, J. H., Beneke, S., & Steinheimer, K. (1998a). *Teacher materials for documenting children's work.* New York: Teachers College Press.

Helm, J. H., Beneke, S., & Steinheimer, K. (1998b). *Windows on learning: Documenting young children's work.* New York: Teachers College Press.

Henderson, A., & Berla, N. (Eds.). (1994). *A new generation of evidence: The family is critical to student achievement.* Washington, DC: Center for Law and Education.

Hendricks, J. (Ed.). (1997). *First steps toward teaching the Reggio way.* Upper Saddle River, NJ: Prentice Hall.

Herberholz, B., & Hanson, L. (1994). *Early childhood art.* Boston, MA: McGraw-Hill.

Illinois STARnet. (2000). *A children's journey: Investigating the fire truck.* Regions I and III. Macomb, IL: Center for Best Practices in Early Childhood Education.

Jablon, J., Marsden, D., Meisels, S., & Dichtelmiller, M. (1994). *Omnibus guidelines: Preschool through third grade.* Ann Arbor, MI: Rebus Planning Associates.

Jones, B., Valdez, G., Norakowski, J., & Rasmussen, C. (1994). *Designing learning and technology for educational reform.* Oakbrook, IL: North Central Regional Educational Laboratory.

Katz, L. G. (1993). *Dispositions, definitions, and implications for early childhood practice.* Champaign, IL: ERIC Clearinghouse on Elementary and Early Childhood Education.

Katz, L. G. (1994). *The project approach.* Champaign, IL: ERIC Clearinghouse on Elementary and Early Childhood Education.

Katz, L. G. (1995). *Talks with teachers of young children: A collection.* Stamford, CT: Ablex.

Katz, L. G., & Chard, S. C. (2000). *Engaging children's minds: The project approach* (2nd ed.). Stamford, CT: Ablex.

Katz, L. G., & Chard, S. C. (1996). *The contribution of documentation to the quality of early childhood education.* Champaign, IL: ERIC Clearinghouse on Elementary and Early Childhood Education.

Katz, L. G., & Chard, S. C. (1997). *Notes from project approach lectures.* Presented at Allerton Park, Montecello, Illinois.

Knapp, M. (Ed.). (1995). *Teaching for meaning in high-poverty classrooms.* New York: Teachers College Press.

LeeKeenan, D., & Edwards, C. (1992). Using the project approach with toddlers. *Young Children, 47*(4), 31–35.

Machado, J. (1995). *Early childhood experiences in language arts: Emerging literacy.* Albany, NY: Delmar.

Marcon, R. A. (1992). Differential effects of three preschool models on inner-city 4-year-olds. *Early Childhood Research Quarterly, 7*(4), 517–530.

Marcon, R. A. (1995). Fourth-grade slump: The cause and cure. *Principal, 74*(5), 6–17, 19–20.

Mayer, M. (1987). *There's an alligator under my bed.* New York: Dial Books for Young Children.

McLaughlin, B. (1995). *Fostering second language development in young children: Principles and practices.* Santa Cruz, CA: National Center for Research on Cultural Diversity and Second Language Learning.

Meisels, S. J., Jabolon, J. R., Marsden, D. B., Dichtelmiller, M. L., Dorfman, A. B., & Steele, D. M. (1994). *An overview: The work sampling system.* Ann Arbor, MI: Rebus Planning Associates.

Miller, L. B., & Bizzell, R. P. (1983). Long-term effects of four preschool programs: Sixth, seventh, and eighth grades. *Child Development, 54*(3), 727–741.

National Association for the Education of Young Children. (1995). *Responding to linguistic and cultural diversity: Recommendations for effective early childhood education.* Washington, DC: Author.

National Association for the Education of Young Children and the International Reading Association. (1998, May). *Learning to read and write: Developmentally appropriate practices for young children.* Washington, DC: National Association for the Education of Young Children.

National Committee on Science Education Standards and Assessment. (1995). *Education standards.* Washington, DC: National Research Council.

Neuman, S., Copple, C., & Bredekamp, S. (2000). *Learning to read and write: Developmentally appropriate practices for young children.* Washington, DC: National Association for the Education of Young Children.

New, R. (1990). Excellent early education: A city in Italy has it! *Young Children, 45*(6), 4–10.

New, R. (1991). Early childhood teacher education in Italy: Reggio Emilia's master plan for "master" teachers. *The Journal of Early Childhood Teacher Education, 12*(37), 3.

Pérez, B., & Torres-Guzmán, M. E. (1995). *Learning in two worlds.* White Plains, NY: Longman.

Rankin, B. (1992). Inviting children's creativity: A story of Reggio Emilia, Italy. *Child Care Information Exchange, No. 85,* 30–35.

Schweinhart, L. (1997). *Child-initiated learning activities for young children living in poverty: ERIC Digest.* Urbana, IL: ERIC Clearinghouse on Elementary and Early Childhood Education.

Smilansky, S., Hagan, J., & Lewis, H. (1988). *Clay in the classroom: Helping children develop cognitive and affective skills for learning.* New York: Teachers College Press.

Smith, C. (1998). Children with "special rights" in the pre-primary schools and infant-toddler centers of Reggio Emilia. In C. Edwards, L. Gandini, & G. Forman (Eds.), *The hundred languages of children: The Reggio Emilia approach—Advanced reflections* (2nd ed.; pp. 199–214). Stamford, CT: Ablex.

Smith, L. (1997). "Open education" revisited: Promise and problems in American educational reform. *Teachers College Record, 99*(2), 371–415.

Smith, N. R., & the Drawing Study Group. (1998). *Observation drawing with children : A framework for teachers.* New York: Teachers College Press.

Snow, C. E., Burns, M. S., & Griffin, P. (1998). *Preventing reading difficulties in young children.* Washington, DC: National Academy Press.

Topal, C. W. (1983). *Children, clay and sculpture*. Worchester, MA: Davis Publications.

Vygotsky, L. S. (1978). *Mind in society: The development of higher mental processes* (M. Cole, V. John-Steiner, S. Scribner, & E. Souberman, Eds. & Trans.). Cambridge, MA: Harvard University Press.

Whitmore, K., & Goodman, Y. M. (1995). Transforming curriculum in language and literacy. In S. Bredekamp & T. Rosegrant (Eds.), *Reaching potentials: Transforming early childhood curriculum and assessment* (pp. 145–166). Washington, DC: National Association for the Education of Young Children.

Wong Fillmore, L. (1985). Second language learning in children: A proposed model. In R. Eshch & J. Provinzano (Eds.), *Issues in English language development*. Rosslyn, VA: National Clearinghouse for Bilingual Education. (ERIC Document No. ED 273 149)

Index

About the Authors

Judy Harris Helm is Associate Professor, National College of Education at National-Louis University, Wheeling Campus. She also assists schools and early childhood programs in integrating research and new methods through her consulting and training company, Best Practices, Inc. She began her career teaching first grade, then taught, directed, and designed early childhood and primary programs as well as training teachers at the community college, undergraduate, and graduate levels. She served on the Task Force for the design of the Valeska Hinton Early Childhood Education Center, a state-of-the-art urban collaboration school for children age 3 through first grade in Peoria, Illinois, where she became Professional Development Coordinator for the school. She is past state president of the Illinois Association for the Education of Young Children.

Dr. Helm is co-author of *Windows on Learning: Documenting Children's Work* published by Teachers College Press. She is editor of *The Project Catalog I and II* published by ERIC.

Lilian G. Katz is Professor Emerita of Early Childhood Education at the University of Illinois (Urbana-Champaign) where she is also Director of the ERIC Clearinghouse on Elementary & Early Childhood Education. Professor Katz is author of more than 100 publications including articles, chapters, and books about early childhood education, teacher education, child development, and parenting.

Dr. Katz was founding editor of the *Early Childhood Research Quarterly*, and served as Editor-in-Chief during its first six years. She is currently Chair of the editorial board of the *International Journal of the Early Years* published in the UK. In 1989 she wrote *Engaging Children's Minds: The Project Approach* (with S. C. Chard), which has served as a model for the project approach. Dr. Katz has lectured in all 50 U.S. states and in 43 countries. She has held visiting posts at universities in Australia, Canada, England, Germany, India, Israel, the West Indies (Barbados campus), and many parts of the United States.

Project
Planning Journal

Name of Teacher _____

Project Title _____

Project Dates _____ to _____

School/Center _____

Age Level _____

Project # _____

Introduction to the Project Planning Journal

The Project Planning Journal serves two purposes. The first purpose is to support and encourage teachers while they are learning how to do a first project. Along with the chapters in this book, *Young Investigators: The Project Approach in the Early Years*, the journal provides step-by-step guidance through the decisions that a teacher has to make in doing a first project with young children. It helps teachers prepare, plan, and implement a project with young investigators in their own classroom. The main task in each phase of the project is presented, questions to consider are listed, and space is reserved for teacher reflection.

A second, unplanned, purpose for the journal was discovered as teachers who already knew how to guide projects with young children began to use it as a convenient way to organize their thinking and record information. It enabled them to keep track of their planning tasks, the events of a project, and their documentation. For busy teachers, it provided reassurance that they were preserving the key information about each project. More important, the journal appears to provide a place and a purpose for reflections. These reflections were often then shared with colleagues.

The Project Planning Journal is designed to be photocopied by teachers to use in various ways. Some teachers put copies into three-ring binders and add additional pages for notes. Some add scrapbook pages for photographs. If they are used for the second and subsequent projects, teachers can build a data bank of their project experiences. This encourages teachers to look back on their own development as teachers guiding projects.

The journal is a guide, a road map for a journey. Projects, like journeys, do not always take the direct route. There may be side roads followed, detours taken that enrich and delight. The flowchart in Chapter 1 (Figure 1.5) is more a road map than a blueprint, as is this journal. It shows the lay of the land, where roads lead and where one might go. It is not like a blueprint for a building that must be carefully and precisely followed. Where the journey goes and where the children and teacher end up is decided by them together.

Phase I: Beginning the Project

Determining Children's Interest and Selecting a Topic

Possible topic emerges → Emerging from child interest **P** OR → Initiated by the teacher →

What general topics appear to interest the children in your classroom?

How did you learn about their interest?
☐ Conversations   ☐ Drawings   ☐ Observations   ☐ Questions   ☐ Parent report

If a student-initiated topic does not emerge, the curriculum can be examined for broad topic areas. Is there an event or learning experience coming that could be used as a starting point? A walk around the school and neighborhood will often result in identifying something in the vicinity that might interest your children.

What are your curriculum goals for the children this year? Attach a list of curriculum goals to your journal. Are there some topics that are both of interest to your children and a part of your curriculum goals?

Select a few topics of interest and apply the criteria for selection of a topic for a project (see Chapter 2). If this topic were to develop into a project, would the experience have value for children?
Will it

____ Help young investigators understand their own experience and environment more fully and accurately?

____ Strengthen the disposition to look closely at phenomena in their environments worthy of appreciation?

____ Provide ample opportunity for children to employ a wide variety of interactive skills and dispositions while conducting the investigation?

____ Provide opportunity for children to develop insight into the functions and limitations of a variety of different media and develop skillfulness in applying the various media to their work?

What topics that your children find of interest meet the criteria for topic selection?

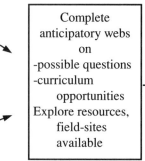

Complete anticipatory webs on
-possible questions
-curriculum opportunities
Explore resources, field-sites available

Make an Anticipatory Planning Web

Make a web to see if the project can be integrated with your curriculum. If you do not have a required curriculum experiment with some of the anticipatory webs described in Chapter 2. If you do have a required curriculum, follow the webbing process described in Chapter 6.

Copy your planning web here.

Teacher Journal: Topic Selection Take time to reflect on your selection of this possible topic. Record your thoughts.

What are your reasons for selecting this topic?

What possible directions could it take?

What content or skills would be strengthened?

What do you know about this topic? What would you like to know about this topic?

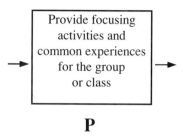

P

Trying Out a Topic and Getting Started

The project can begin in several ways: Children express an interest, teacher introduces a topic, or a topic is agreed upon by children and teacher (Katz & Chard, 1989). For young children, it is helpful to spend some time introducing the topic.

Topic: **Date Phase I Began:**

Establish Common Ground

The main idea is to establish a common ground among the children by pooling the information, ideas, and experiences they already have about a topic. Build a shared perspective. During preliminary discussions, the teacher encourages talking about the topic, playing, and depicting current understanding in many ways. (Katz & Chard, 1989, p. 82)

The younger the children and the more diverse the group, the more time the teacher may need to spend creating a common understanding. Teachers may provide several experiences for children relating to the topic. Children will need enough knowledge about the topic to develop questions for investigation.

What event can be used to focus the children's attention on this topic?
☐ Book   ☐ Video   ☐ Related objects   ☐ Discussion   ☐ Dramatic play

Notes/Results:

P Is there an opportunity to involve parents in focusing events?

What do the children already know about this topic? How can their knowledge be recorded?
For ideas on how to access children's prior knowledge, see Chapter 2.
☐ Web   ☐ List of questions   ☐ Drawings/constructions   ☐ Recording discussions

Notes/Results:

Extend Children's Interest and Build a Common Vocabulary

What resources can be used to stimulate interest and clarify questions?
☐ Books   ☐ Construction materials   ☐ Visitors   ☐ Artifacts   ☐ Parent contributions

Notes/Results:

How are the children showing what they already know about the topic? How are they beginning to explore the topic?
☐ Drawings/sketches   ☐ Paintings   ☐ Constructions   ☐ Play   ☐ Language products

What can be done to encourage representation?

Notes/Results:

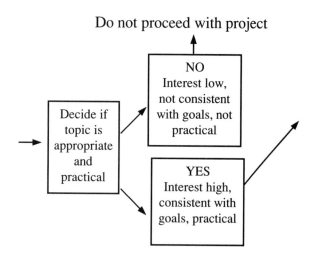

Do not proceed with project

Deciding If the Topic Is Appropriate for a Project

If this topic were to develop into a project, how practical would it be for a project for young children?

Is it a topic that
___ Is more concrete than abstract?
___ Involves an abundance of first-hand, direct experiences and real objects that young investigators can manipulate?
___ Is easily related to their prior experiences?
___ Has related sites nearby that can be conveniently visited and even revisited?
___ Young children can research with minimal assistance from adults? Can it be researched without relying only on secondary sources like books, internet or video?
___ Children can represent what they know and learn by using skills and techniques appropriate for their age?
___ Is culturally relevant to the children and their families?

Is this topic still a topic of interest?
☐ No, because children's interest in this topic has waned.
☐ Yes.

Does the topic have merit for curriculum integration?
☐ No, it does not fit curriculum goals.
☐ Yes.

If the answer to either of the above questions is no, you can continue to explore the topic as a teacher directed unit or move on to other topics. Wait for a better topic for a project.

If both answers are yes—the children are interested and this has promise of being a valuable learning experience—then proceed with the project.

Plan for Documentation

Take time now to think about documentation.

Review the following list of ways to document. For more information on documentation see Chapter 6 and consult *Windows on Learning: Documenting Young Children's Work* (Helm, Beneke, & Steinheimer, 1998a, 1998b).

What types of documentation can be used for this project? Come back to this page often during the project. Write down what has been collected for each type.

☐ Project narratives: Telling the story

☐ Observations of child development: Watching the child

☐ Checklists of knowledge and skills in curriculum

☐ Anecdotal notes

☐ Individual portfolios

☐ Individual and group products:
   Written language products: Signs, letters, books
   Verbal language products
   Webs and lists
   Pictures
   Representational pictures: Time 1 and Time 2 pictures, symbolic pictures
   Music and movement
   Constructions: Play environments, sculpture, blocks, or building toys

☐ Self-reflections of students

Are there characteristics of this topic that make one type of documentation more effective than another?

Are there school or center personnel who can be asked to help with documentation?

Are there parents who can help with documentation (i.e., photographing, taking dictation, videotaping)?

This documentation planning sheet should be completed as the project progresses (see Chapter 5). "Collection task" refers to taking photos, writing down conversations, and so forth. If the teacher aide does this task, then plan for someone else to cover the teacher aide's task that would normally be done at this time. For example, a parent may prepare the snack. Think ahead and prepare materials and equipment.

Anticipated Project Events	Possible Types of Documentation	Equipment or Materials Needed	Collection Task Assigned To	Coverage of Collector's Tasks

Determining What Children Know and What They Want to Find Out

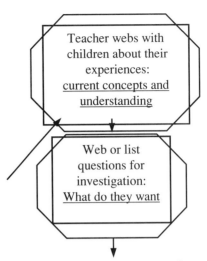

Teacher webs with children about their experiences: <u>current concepts and understanding</u>

Web or list questions for investigation: <u>What do they want</u>

In a large or small group, talk with children about what they know about the topic. What concepts and understanding do they already have about the topic? How will you record it?

☐ Webs　　　　　☐ Lists

Notes/Results:

With the children, record what they want to know about the topic. What initial questions have been generated for possible research?

☐ Webs　　　　　☐ Lists

Notes/Results:

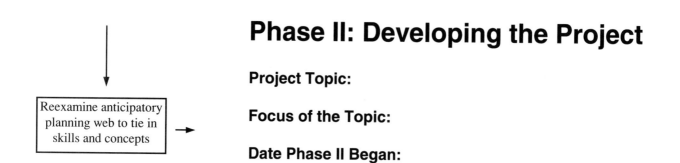

Phase II: Developing the Project

Project Topic:

Focus of the Topic:

Date Phase II Began:

Reexamining the Instructional Planning Web
Now that a topic has been selected, reexamine the planning web. What curriculum goals will integrate into the project? Are there experiences that should be provided at times other than project work times? If the topic has changed significantly from the anticipatory web and there is a required curriculum, consult Chapter 6.

Teacher Journal: Looking Ahead What can the children gain from this experience? What content and skill development do I hope to see? What dispositions do I hope will be strengthened?

Preparing for Investigation

The emphasis during this phase is on introducing new information and finding answers to questions. This phase can include visiting field-sites, talking with visitors who bring real objects to the classroom, and examining books, photographs, or artifacts. Children are encouraged to follow their interests and find answers to their questions.

How can the investigation become focused?

☐ Discussion   ☐ New web   ☐ List of questions   ☐ Assigned tasks

Notes/Results:

What additional resources should be brought into the classroom to enable and support in-depth study?

☐ Books   ☐ Construction materials   ☐ Visitors   ☐ Artifacts   ☐ **P**arent contributions

Notes/Results:

What skills might the children need help with? These skills are described in Chapter 3 with suggestions for practicing and integrating these skills. These skills are also learned <u>during</u> the project.

☐ How to pose a question to an adult
☐ How to tally data
☐ Observing and talking about what they observed
☐ Observational drawing and field sketching
☐ Taking photographs
☐ Using construction tools and materials such as tape, glue, staplers
☐ Using clay

How can the children best be prepared for field-site experience?

☐ Discussion   ☐ Practicing skills   ☐ Reminders   ☐ Rehearsal

Notes/Results:

Planning for Field-Site Visits

Arrange Transportation
Do I need to arrange for transportation to a site? Do I need permission slips from parents?

Communicate with Field-Site Personnel
How will I prepare the field-site personnel to maximize investigation opportunities for my children?
☐ Phone call ☐ Pre-trip visit by teacher ☐ Reminder letter ☐ "How We Are Learning" handout
Checklist for discussion with site personnel (see Chapter 3 on preparing site personnel)
_____ Safety issues involved in this site visit
_____ Importance of child investigation
_____ Importance of direct first-hand experiences
_____ Importance of real objects, especially those with which children can interact
_____ Overview of what the children currently know and understand
_____ Overview of what they are interested in learning (share some of the questions children might ask)
_____ Explanation of how children will record what they see, what they think, and what they found out: tape recording? video? clipboards? writing? photographing?
_____ Brainstorming possible items or scenes that students may sketch or record
_____ Artifacts (tools, equipment, products, etc.) that can be borrowed and kept in the classroom for further investigation
_____ Importance of having a guide or host with experience in communicating with young children

Notes from discussion:

Plan and Prepare for Adult Helpers/Chaperones P
How many children will go on the visit?_____ How many adults are needed? _____
What preparations should adult helpers have?
☐ Phone call ☐ Request letter ☐ Meeting ☐ Reminder note ☐ "How We Are Learning" handout
Checklist to cover with adult helpers:
_____ Warning about safety issues involved in this site visit or expert visitor visit
_____ Importance of child investigation, that questions will come from students
_____ Overview of what the children know, understand, and what they are interested in learning
_____ Importance of children interacting with real objects and using their senses
_____ Explanation of how they can help children record what they learn (tape recording, video, writing, photographing)
_____ Explanation of importance of seeing adults model drawing, writing, or recording
_____ Possible items or scenes that children may sketch or record
_____ Artifacts (tools, equipment, products, etc.) that may be brought back or borrowed for further investigation
_____ Time schedule
_____ Information about particular children who might require special assistance

Organize the Children

Organize the Children

How will children be organized for the experience?

☐ Children assigned to specific adult ☐ Groups with a specific task ☐ One large group

How will responsibility for children be assigned to adult helpers? List adults who are helping and list children by groups.

Gather Materials and Supplies for the Field-Site Visit

Materials and supplies needed:

____ Clipboards

____ Recording equipment ☐ camera ☐ camcorder ☐ tape recorder

____ Paper, pencils, art materials

____ Bags, boxes, or other containers for materials collected

____ Other

Teacher Journal: Field-Site Visit Write a narrative about what happened during the field trip. Where did the children go? What did the children see and do? With whom did they interact? What were the highlights of the experience?

Arranging for Visiting Experts

Will the visitor come into the classroom? Do I need to schedule a room or space?

Prepare for field work and expert visitors

Communicate with the Visiting Expert
How will I prepare the expert visitor to maximize the opportunities for investigation for my children? (See also Chapter 3)

☐ Phone call to the visitor   ☐ Reminder letter   ☐ "How We Are Learning" handout

Checklist for discussion with visiting experts.

_____ Safety issues involved in this visit. Will items brought into the classroom be safe for children to explore?

_____ Importance of child investigation

_____ Importance of direct first-hand experiences

_____ Importance of real objects, especially those with which children can interact

_____ Overview of what the children currently know and understand

_____ Overview of what they are interested in learning (share some of the questions children might ask)

_____ Explanation of how children will be recording what they see, what they think, and what they found out (tape recording, video, clipboards, writing, photographing)

_____ Brainstorming possible items for the expert to bring that children may sketch or record

_____ Artifacts (tools, equipment, products, etc.) that can be borrowed and kept in the classroom for further investigation

_____ Importance of using language that young children can understand

Notes from discussion:

Plan for Adult Helpers
Would it be helpful to have additional adults in the classroom when the visit occurs?

How many adults are needed? _____

What preparations should adult helpers have?

☐ Phone call ☐ Request letter ☐ Meeting ☐ Reminder note ☐ "How We Are Learning" handout

Checklist to cover with adult helpers:

_____ Warning about safety issues involved in this visit

_____ Importance of child investigation, that questions will come from students

_____ Overview of what the children currently know and what they are interested in learning

_____ Importance of children's interacting with real objects and using their senses

_____ Explanation of how they can help students record what they learn (tape recording, video, clipboards, writing, photographing)

_____ Explanation of importance of seeing adults model drawing, writing, or recording

_____ Time schedule

_____ Information about particular children who might require special assistance.

Gather Materials and Supplies Needed When the Visiting Expert Comes
_____ Clipboards

_____ Recording equipment   ☐ camera   ☐ camcorder   ☐ tape recorder

_____ Paper, pencils, art materials

How will children be organized for the experience?
☐ Children assigned to specific adult ☐ Groups with a specific task ☐ One large group
☐ Children individually approach or observe the visitor

How will responsibilities be assigned to adult helpers? If adult helpers will be assisting with groups of children, list the groups here.

Teacher Journal: Expert Visitor Write a narrative about what happened during the expert's visit. What did children see and do? What were the highlights of the experience?

Representing What Was Learned

How will children review their experiences and field work?
- ☐ Discuss sketches ☐ Time 1/Time 2 drawings ☐ Review photos
- ☐ Dictate experience ☐ Revise webs ☐ Answer questions on list →
- ☐ Scrapbook ☐ Display

Other:

> Represent what was learned through writing, drawing, construction, dancing, and dramatic play
>
> **P**

How can children be encouraged to use secondary sources?
- ☐ Introduce books ☐ Add to choices in room ☐ Encourage play, creation of play environment

How can the children represent what they have learned about the topic?
- ☐ Drawings/sketches ☐ Paintings ☐ Constructions ☐ Play ☐ Language products

What do I need to do to encourage representation?

How can the following experiences be provided through this project?
- ☐ Problem solving: What can children figure out on their own?

- ☐ Application of construction skills such as taping, gluing, organizing materials.

- ☐ Working together as a group.

□ Using a variety of ways to represent what they are learning and to communicate, such as drawing, building, dramatic play, writing, constructing, musical expression, and so forth.

Teacher Journal Write a narrative about the children's dispositions and the development of investigation skills. What dispositions are you seeing expressed during their project work? Are the children actively engaged in the project?

Revisiting the Children's Web and List of Questions

```
Revisit web or re-web
indicate what was learned,
identify new questions,
repeat investigation and
representation.
```

What have children learned? Did they find the answers to their questions?

Are there new questions for investigation? How might they be answered?

What would be helpful for the children to have?
- ☐ More resources such as books
- ☐ Additional experts to visit
- ☐ Additional field-site visits
    - ☐ Same site revisited
    - ☐ Different site
- ☐ Revisiting of documentation of field site
- ☐ More representation opportunities

What additional experiences can be provided?

Determine When to Culminate the Project
- ☐ Are the children satisfied with their new knowledge?
- ☐ Would further investigation require skills the children do not have (such as advanced reading and writing)?
- ☐ Are children just losing interest in the topic?

If the answers are yes, then the project is probably ready for culmination.

Debrief,
plan culminating event
for students to share,
tell the story of
the project

P

Phase III: Concluding the Project

In the third phase children bring work to completion and summarize what has been learned. It is important that children are able to "elaborate what they have learned so that its meaning is enhanced and made personal" (Katz & Chard, 1989, p. 84).

Sharing with Others What We Have Learned

What evidence of children's learning can be gathered and discussed with them?
☐ Drawings/sketches   ☐ Paintings   ☐ Constructions   ☐ Language products
☐ Final webs   ☐ Lists   ☐ Play

Discuss the project with the children. What do the children think they have learned?

With whom would they like to share their project?

How might the children share what they have learned?
☐ Exhibit
☐ Role-play in play environment
☐ Make histories of the project
☐ Write reports
☐ Plays, dramas, music
☐ Make individual scrapbooks or files
☐ School presentation
☐ Open house for parents
☐ Presentation for parents
☐ Take home books
☐ Community displays

Complete the
Culminating Event
or
Activities

P

What types of documentation have I used to document this project? Review the following list of varieties of ways to document (see Chapter 5; also Helm et al., 1998a, 1998b).

☐ Project narratives
☐ Observations of child development
☐ Checklists of knowledge and skills in curriculum
☐ Anecdotal notes
☐ Individual portfolios
☐ Individual and group products:
      Written language products: signs, letters, books
      Verbal language products
      Webs and lists
      Pictures
      Representational pictures: Time 1/Time 2 pictures, symbolic pictures
      Music and movement
      Constructions: Play environments, sculpture, blocks, or building toys
☐ Self-reflections of children

Consider Next Project
Is there another topic that has emerged for further investigation?

Would this topic be a topic to investigate now or at a later time?

P

Teacher Journal Review the project. What have you learned about topic selection? Was this a good topic? Why did it work or not work for children's investigation?

Review page 12 (Phase II). Did children gain the content knowledge and skills that you hoped they would?

What did you learn about Phase I?

What did you learn about Phase II?

What did you learn about Phase III?

What would you do differently in the next project?

What suggestions do you have for other teachers working with the same age group or topic?

Evaluate Engagement in Learning

Apply the concepts of engaged learning to your project (see Chapter 5).

1. Did the children take responsibility for their own work or activity?

___ Did they show that they have a voice in what they study?

___ Did they take charge of the learning experience and explain or show the teacher what they wanted to do?

2. Were children absorbed and engrossed in their work?

___ Did they find satisfaction and pleasure in their work?

___ Were they developing a taste for solving problems and understanding ideas or concepts?

3. Were children strategic learners?

___ Were they developing problem-solving strategies and skills?

___ Did they apply what they learned in one experience to a similar experience?

4. Were the children becoming increasingly collaborative?

___ Did they work with other children?

___ Could they talk about their ideas to others?

___ Were they fair-minded in dealing with those who disagreed with them?

___ Did they offer each other support, suggestions, and encouragement?

___ Did they recognize their strengths and the strengths of others?

5. Were tasks in the projects challenging and integrative?

___ Were they complex, requiring sustained amounts of time over days or even weeks?

___ Did tasks require children to stretch their thinking and social skills in order to be successful?

___ Were children learning how literacy, math, science, and communication skills are helpful?

___ Were all children encouraged to ask hard questions, to define problems, and to take part in conversations?

6. Is children's work from the project being used to assess their learning?

___ Is there documentation of how children constructed knowledge and created artifacts to represent their learning?

___ Is there documentation of achievement of the goals of the curriculum?

___ Does the documentation include individual and group efforts?

___ Does the documentation make visible children's dispositions in the project such as to solve problems, to ask questions, and so forth?

___ Does the documentation include drafts as well as final products?

___ Were children involved in the documentation process and encouraged to reflect on the documentation?

___ Were children encouraged to generate criteria, such as what makes a good observational drawing or a good question?

7. *Did you, as a teacher, facilitate and guide the children's work?*

      ___Did you provide a rich environment, rich experiences, and activities?

      ___Did you encourage sharing of knowledge and responsibility?

      ___Did you adjust the level of information and support based on children's needs?

      ___Did you help children link new information to prior knowledge?

      ___Did you help children develop strategies to find out what they want to know?

      ___Did you model and coach?

      ___Did you feel like a co-learner and co-investigator with the children?

Teacher Journal Write a final narrative on this project. Was this project an engaged learning experience for you and your children? What might you have done differently to increase engagement? Closing thoughts:

How We Are Learning:
An Introduction to the Project Approach

What is the project approach?

The project approach is a method of teaching in which an in-depth study of a particular topic is conducted by a child or a group of children.

How is it different from others ways of learning?

Our children study one topic for a long time period. The topic is selected partly because they were interested in it and it is meaningful to them and their lives. The children will go into great depth and often at a level higher than many adults would expect for this. The teacher integrates content knowledge like math, reading, and science into the project.

How is a project planned?

The children make many of their own plans with the teacher's help. Plans usually include an on site visit and/or interviews with experts. An expert is anyone who knows a great deal about the topic of study.

How will children learn?

Children use a variety of resources to find answers to their questions. These include traditional resources like books. They also conduct in-depth investigations on site visits. The children plan questions for interviews and have assigned tasks for trips or for interviewing experts. They make field notes and draw or write on site. They make plans for building structures and play environments that will help them sort out what they are learning about the topic.

Children do their own problem solving with the teacher structuring problems and assisting in finding solutions and resources. Children will redraw and rewrite as their knowledge grows. Some of the ways that they will record their learning are project books, posters, murals, artwork, graphs, charts, constructions, and journals.

How does the teacher know if children are learning?

The teacher collects children's work, observes what they do, and analyzes their work. This is called documentation. The curriculum goals of the school or center are reviewed and documentation is planned to be sure that children are learning concepts and skills specified in the goals. Often a display will be prepared that shows what students are learning.

Is this the only way these children are learning?

The project approach is one way among a variety of ways that children learn. The project integrates much of the same knowledge and skills presented in more formal ways in the classroom. Projects have the added advantage of providing an opportunity for children to apply and use what they are learning as they solve problems and share what they know. It provides opportunities for developing group skills such as working with others and challenges children to think, which supports brain development.

How can others help with projects?

Realize that children have their own questions and are learning to use you and many resources to find answers. Take their questions seriously, and listen to what they have to say. Provide space and opportunities for them to draw or photograph what they are studying. Children learn best when many senses are involved so anything that they can touch, see up close, or hear is helpful. Things that can be borrowed for study in the classroom are valued and appreciated, especially parts of machines, tools, samples of products, and so forth. We hope you will follow up, view our documentation, and find out how children have processed what they have learned from this project.